ALLEN BARGFR

AND CECILY MAK

BERKLEE PRESS

MUSIC LAW IN THE DIGITAL AGE

Edited by Jonathan Feist

Berklee Press

Vice President: David Kusek
Dean of Continuing Education: Debbie Cavalier
Chief Operating Officer: Robert F. Green
Managing Editor: Jonathan Feist
Editorial Assistants: Mina Cho, Yousun Choi, Martin Fowler, Emily Goldstein, Claudia Obser
Cover Designer: Kathy Kikkert

ISBN: 978-0-87639-099-3

1140 Boylston Street
Boston, MA 02215-3693 USA
(617) 747-2146

Visit Berklee Press Online at
www.berkleepress.com

DISTRIBUTED BY

HAL•LEONARD®
CORPORATION
7777 W. BLUEMOUND RD. P.O. BOX 13819
MILWAUKEE, WISCONSIN 53213

Visit Hal Leonard Online at
www.halleonard.com

"If music be the food of love, play on, give me excess of it."

—William Shakespeare

For my parents, Allen

For David, Cecily

CONTENTS

AUTHORS' NOTE

This book is designed to serve as a reference guide. It is not intended or designed to serve as a substitute for legal advice. Due to rapid changes in industry law, customs, technology, and legislation, some parts of this book may be outdated even upon publication. The authors and publisher make no warranties as to the information contained in this text, and assume no liability if a reader acts upon the information contained herein. If legal advice is required, please consult the services of an attorney or other qualified professional.

ACKNOWLEDGMENTS

From Allen: I want to thank and acknowledge the following people for their inspiration and help on this project: My parents, for their love and support. Derek Crownover, for pushing me to continue and the oft-needed advice. Rob Gabriel, for listening to me talk about this project incessantly for months. Everyone at the Music Business/Management Department at Berklee College of Music for their support of my career. And Cecily Mak, for working diligently with me for over two years to make this project a reality.

From Cecily: It has been a great privilege to work with Allen on this project since the idea was born in 2007. I know that we have learned a lot since we started. I also must thank the many people who have supported and inspired the evolution of my career in this field. My METaL (Music, Entertainment, Technology, and the Law) crew, particularly Jon Blaufarb, David Marglin, Zahavah Levine, and Tuhin Roy have been supportive, inspiring, and at times, entertaining (you know who you are). The legal and business teams at RealNetworks and Rhapsody America continue to push yet empower me; I would not have been able to contribute to this book without the years of experience and solid mentorship and support of these companies. I also must thank University of California Hastings College of the Law for allowing me to bring the Digital Media Law Seminar to the school at a time when many of the reviewing faculty members needed to ask what "digital media law" actually is. I also must extend my most heartfelt gratitude to my many guest lecturers and many students. You are the primary inspiration behind this book for me; I appreciate your ongoing questions and the inspiration you provide. Last but not least, words cannot express the gratitude and love I feel for my husband David and our young son Xander. You continue to support me in ways that I couldn't have imagined; thank you for making it possible for me to play the many roles I do.

Together we would like to express our gratitude to everyone at Berklee Press and the Music Business/Management Department of the Berklee College of Music. A special thanks goes to Adam Parness for his meticulous proofreading and corrections. We also note our appreciation and admiration for Asha Jameson for her excellent work as our research assistant, and Lisa Liu and Korey Anvaripour for their proofreading support.

INTRODUCTION

The idea for this book emerged when we realized that there was no comprehensive and accurate reference guide for online music distribution and the legalities behind it. Both practicing attorneys with some background in academia (Cecily as an adjunct at the UC Hastings College of the Law, and Allen as full time faculty at the Berklee College of Music), we saw a need for a guide for our students as well. As a result, we have devised this book to direct and support our colleagues, students, and anyone interested in the music industry through the muddy waters of the convergence of technology and music.

Formidable outside forces, such as the birth of a new technology, can forever alter arts and culture in our world. The advent of the Internet and the MP3, as well as digital recording technology, have caused a dramatic paradigm shift in the control and delivery of creative assets in the past fifteen years. Entire catalogs of content are now traded more quickly than a register could ring up a sale at a record store in the past. As online outlets grow and tools for distribution and consumption change, gaps in copyright (the law that protects artistic works and allows creators to control the exploitation of their works) continue to emerge, and courts are left to apply decades-old law to unanticipated situations. New legislation is introduced every year to update the copyright code, but as each stakeholder successfully lobbies to keep its current position intact, there are few significant changes, and the status quo remains the order of the day.

On the other side of the debate, the "copyleft" movement seems to argue for the extinguishment of copyright altogether for an alleged greater cultural good. Leaders of this movement point to remarkably creative works that are outright illegal due to inclusion of unlicensed content. In their defense, there are entire genres of music and active creative "remix" communities whose work is at best stifled by the difficulty and costs associated with complying with current copyright law.

On the business side of things, online piracy continues to eat into the sales of recorded music, and CD sales continue their downward spiral. However, while there is much debate about the future of the music industry, one thing remains clear: music consumption has never been higher. With music surrounding us in television, film, video games, satellite radio, and the ability to carry our entire music collection in our pocket, we listen and consume more than ever.

In the coming pages, you will learn the basics of copyright law and policy as it exists today, and how copyright applies to music. We'll look at the revenue sources for both songwriters and artists, and examine the different models for digital distribution. The final pages will provide reference resources. Hopefully, you'll walk away with an understanding of the basics of music and copyright in the digital age. By then, we may already be rewriting this manuscript to include all of the changes in law, policy, and the industry that have taken place since this went to press!

PART I

Introduction to Music Law

CHAPTER 1

History of the Music Industry and Copyright Law

When one thinks of the music industry, thoughts quickly turn to thrilling live performances, gripping albums, and creative marketing techniques, not tediously negotiated contracts or large-scale litigation. However, few industries are as reliant upon compliance with applicable law (including contracts) to derive income as the recorded music industry. The emergence of the original Napster in the late 1990s shone a glaring spotlight on the industry's dependence on lawful distribution models. It was via this end-user revolution that millions of consumers became adept at circumventing long-established distribution methods and long standing copyright laws. (Copyright is the right of an author of a creative work to control the uses of the work and financially benefit from its exploitation.) As we continue to evolve in today's evermore-networked world, the application and enforcement of current copyright law becomes increasingly critical to the evolution and strength of the entire music and entertainment industry.

MUSIC FORMATS

Recorded music has a long history of distribution via a variety of changing formats and media. In the 1870s, the cylinder emerged as the first recording technology. Thomas Edison then captured the first recorded human voice in 1877 and was issued a patent for his recording technique that same year. The infant record industry began shortly thereafter with the proliferation of device manufacturers and music promoters. By the turn of the century, record labels were springing up, and music as a business began to flourish. In 1913, flat discs started to outgrow cylinders as media for recorded music, and in 1914, ASCAP (the American Society of Composers, Authors and Publishers) was founded to collect public performances fees under the newly enacted 1909 copyright law. Sales of prerecorded music grew quickly in parallel; in fact, sales revenues were nearly $1.2 billion in 1921, using 2009 dollars.

The cylinder was quickly followed by the gramophone as a popular tool for playing recorded music. The Victrola gramophone was released in 1906, and in 1930, the Gramophone Company and the Columbia Gramophone Company merged to become Electrical and Musical Industries (EMI), which today is one of the four remaining major label distributors for recorded music in the United States. The year 1903 brought the first release of prerecorded music on disc records on the Monarch Record Label.

The development of radio, at around the same time as the emergence of recorded music, served to promote the listening of music and brought that music directly into people's homes from distant places. Initially a two-way communications tool for the

Fig. 1.1. Edison Records made black wax cylinders

military and marine navigation, radio was born in the late 1800s and early 1900s, but did not emerge as a commercial product until the 1920s. In 1895, scientists Guglielmo Marconi, Heinrich Hertz, and Alexander Popov conducted experiments and demonstrations of communication through wireless devices, and in 1906, Reginald Fessenden in Massachusetts made the first audio radio broadcast ever, including himself playing the violin and reading the Bible. With all of these changes afoot, no longer was music something seen only live, but rather a portable and transmittable commodity.

At first, radio was seen as a competitor to the recorded music industry. Similar to the recent decline in sales resulting from the distribution of music over the Internet, in the early days of radio, recorded music sales fell rapidly and experts predicted the demise of the then bustling recorded music industry, as people substituted listening to the radio for the purchase of recorded music. As Stan Liebowitz noted in his 2004 study of the impact of radio on recorded music:

> *The recording industry underwent a devastating decline shortly after the advent of radio. Even some commentators who assign the cause of the recording industry's decline to radio's emergence believe that the major impact of radio on record sales changed from substitution to exposure, and that radio now enhances sales of recordings.*[1]

Many analysts believe that the fall in record sales, from $75 million in 1929 to $26 million in 1938 (with a low point of $5 million in 1933) was partially due to the introduction of radio, although we must assume sales were also affected by the economic stresses associated with the Great Depression. In the end, however, radio's ability to introduce the public to new music made it become one of the greatest marketing tools for the sale of recorded music, not a competitor.

Some compare the decline in record sales following the introduction of radio with the recent fall due to the availability of music for free online; however, we can differentiate the two phenomena based on their relative substitutive natures. While radio "request" shows became common in the 1950s, with listeners calling stations

---

1 Liebowitz, Stan J. "The Elusive Symbiosis: The Impact of Radio on the Record Industry." *Review of Economic Research on Copyright Issues.* 1: (2004), 93–118.

and requesting songs, the requested song was not always played, and if it was, rarely was it played immediately. Conversely, the availability of songs for illegal download on the Internet *does* substitute for the purchase and immediate consumption of recorded music, since potential consumers can immediately fulfill a desire for a certain song. Liebowitz noted that:

> *The substitution effect, at first blush, seems likely to be stronger in the case of MP3 downloads than for radio play of music due to the fact that downloads provide the listener with a copy of the song that has virtually identical attributes to the purchased version. There would seem to be little reason to purchase the song under these circumstances, leading to a very strong substitution effect. Listening to the radio does not leave the listener with a useable alternative that can substitute for the purchase of prerecorded music.[2]*

So while the radio and the new songs it could bring to the home initially captivated listeners, it ultimately could not satisfy consumers' demand for specific music.

Other media for recorded music developed over time, with the introduction by Columbia of 33 rpm 12-inch discs in 1948, and the release of stereo LPs in late 1950s. Within the 1960s, audiocassettes, eight-track cartridges, and Dolby noise reduction all entered the fray as well. By the late 1970s, the leap to digital was underway, largely led by Philips, and in 1979 Philips and Sony Technology teamed up to design the new digital audio disc.[3] A task force, led by Kees Immink and Toshitad Doi, progressed the research into laser technology and optical discs that had been started by Philips in 1977.[4] Philips and Sony eventually agreed on a standard sampling rate of 44.1 kHz and 16-bit audio, and the disc ended up with a 12 cm diameter due to Sony's insistence that a disc hold all of Beethoven's 9th symphony, which clocked in at 74 minutes. The CD ultimately had its first commercial release in Germany in 1982 with ABBA's *The Visitors*.

Despite initial opposition by U.S. record labels who thought the format would confuse customers and ruin the business, CDs

---

2 Liebowitz, Stan J. "The Elusive Symbiosis: The Impact of Radio on the Record Industry." *Review of Economic Research on Copyright Issues*. 1: (2004)

3 Pohlmann, Ken C., *The Compact Disc Handbook*, 2nd Edition, A-R Editions Inc., 1992

4 http://news.bbc.co.uk, "How the CD was Developed," August 2007.

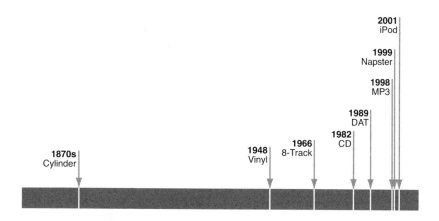

eventually became the standard media for recorded music, with their full digital sound and no loss of frequencies or tape hiss. Labels began to gorge themselves on added revenue, which resulted from consumers' replacement of their recorded music libraries with the CD format, and in 2000, global CD sales peaked at 2.455 billion units.

In 1989, Sony released Digital Audio Tape (DAT) technology. Despite the fact that DAT never took off as a widely used medium, it was immensely important in the development of recorded music distribution, because it was the first technology to allow re-recording of music multiple times without significant loss of sound quality. Not surprisingly, its debut as a consumer product touched off a firestorm of piracy concerns, and despite the fact that Sony was unable to build DAT into a widely used format, the technology ultimately resulted in the passage of the Audio Home Recording Act of 1992. We will discuss the Act in chapter 2.

A Game Changer

A transformation began with the development and emergence of the commercial Internet in the 1990s, which, with its new high-speed broadband capabilities, brought the ability to send and share large data files quickly and easily. Nearly simultaneously, the German company Fraunhofer-Gesellschaft developed MP3 technology, which allowed for the compression of audio files into manageable sizes. MP3s use a lossy compression algorithm designed to greatly reduce the amount of data required to represent the audio recording and yet maintain the sound of a faithful reproduction. It works by

Fig. 1.2. MP3 Files Are Widely Compatible and Easily Transferred

reducing the accuracy of certain parts of sound that are deemed beyond the auditory resolution ability of most people, resulting in a file that is 8 to 10 percent of the size of the CD file created from the original audio source. All developers of MP3 encoders and decoders/players now pay a licensing fee to Fraunhofer.

Fig. 1.3. Fiber Optic Cables. Fiber optic cables began bringing broadband access to life in the 1990s.

The public quickly realized that a digital copy of a song in MP3 format, at about 3 to 5 megabytes in size, could easily be shared over data lines. A song could now be sent via the Internet in as little as one minute, and sites emerged such as MP3.com, which allowed independent bands to post and share music. (MP3.com later became one of the first targets of music industry lawsuits, which alleged the site was making copyrighted material available for free.)

Free-for-All?

In 1999, Shawn Fanning, then a student at Northeastern University in Boston, developed a computer program called Napster, which took advantage of the combination of MP3 and broadband technologies to allow "peer-to-peer" (P2P) file sharing. Via a simple search interface, Napster enabled users to search for and share files across the Internet, and music, newly encoded as MP3s, became easily traded. Fanning testified in a congressional hearing of his idea:

> I began designing and programming a real-time system for locating MP3 files of other users on the Internet. I designed the Napster software to find MP3s because they are the most compressed format (in consideration of bandwidth) and they were very popular at the time.

However, unlike MP3.com, which provided files from its central server, Napster merely provided a search service—a central database that connected users with other users who were online and "sharing" their MP3 files. The files went directly from one user's computer to another, bypassing any Napster equipment. The program's popularity grew phenomenally fast, and users shared over 1.7 billion songs in November of 2000.

Thus, a mere consumer, rather than a music or technology company, became the designer of the next wave of the music industry, and broadband Internet access, MP3 technology, and Fanning's computer program converged to create an easy way to share music files without any requirement of payment for the copyrighted material. Record sales were immediately impacted, with sales declining over a half billion dollars in 2000.

The Recording Industry Association of America (RIAA), which represents the interests of major and independent record labels, sued Fanning and Napster in 2000 for contributory copyright infringement, requesting the statutorily allowed maximum $100,000 in damages for each copyrighted song that had been traded on the service, which equaled hundreds of millions of dollars. Napster argued that because the files were never on Napster's servers, and they merely provided an interface enabling direct connections between users, they were not infringing on any intellectual property and that their service should fall under the safe harbor protections of the Digital Millennium Copyright Act (the "DMCA"). Napster lost the original ruling in the summer of 2000, but continued to operate pending an appeal. However, the appeals court in San Francisco issued an injunction in February of 2001 that required Napster to stop allowing the sharing of copyrighted material. (We will analyze the Napster ruling in more detail in chapter 8.)

Because Napster did not have a mechanism to effectively filter out copyrighted material from other authorized works, the injunction essentially forced the complete shutdown of the company. However, other peer-to-peer sharing services such as Kazaa and Morpheus appeared and took its place, and the music industry was forever altered. Karl Greenfeld noted in *Time Magazine* that:

> *Love it or hate it, that's what Napster has done: changed the world. It has forced record companies to rethink their business models and record-company lawyers and recording artists to defend their intellectual property. It has forced purveyors of "content," like Time Warner, parent company of Time Magazine, to wonder what content will even be in the near future. Napster and Fanning have come to personify the bloody intersection where commerce, culture, and the First Amendment are colliding. On behalf of five media companies, the Recording Industry Association of America (RIAA) has sued Napster, claiming the Web site and Fanning's program are facilitating the theft of intellectual property. Most likely the blueprint for the future of the entertainment industry will be drawn from this ruling.[5]*

Though labels were successful in their fight against Napster, attempts to close individual file sharing sites through litigation was costly and seemed fruitless, with new services emerging continuously. In the summer of 2003, the RIAA began a different

---

5 Greenfeld, Karl Taro. "Meet the Napster." *Time Magazine*. 2 October 2000.

enforcement effort: targeting individuals who traded music online with civil lawsuits. Relying on the DMCA to issue subpoenas to Internet service providers and force them to divulge the identities of certain users, the association, in a very high profile attempt to threaten and scare consumers engaged in illicit downloading, directly sued individuals who had downloaded pirated music online. Between 2003 and the summer of 2008, when the RIAA signalled a departure from this strategy, the group sued approximately 30,000 downloaders, seeking statutory damages up to $150,000 per violation. Some alleged offenders chose to settle, for an average of about $12,000, and others have fought vigorously in court. (In August of 2008, the RIAA publicly announced a shift in strategy, now focusing on collaboration with Internet service providers (ISPs) to try to stop online piracy through a variety of other initiatives.)

THE RECORDING INDUSTRY ASSOCIATION OF AMERICA

The Recording Industry Association of America (RIAA) was formed in 1952, with the initial purpose of administering the RIAA equalization curve, a standard of frequency response applied to vinyl records during manufacturing and playback.

However, the RIAA is now one of the largest lobbying groups in the U.S., with 1600 member labels doing over $11.5 billion in sales revenue in 2007. Its members account for nearly 90 percent of recorded music sold in the United States. While the RIAA has continued to participate in creating and administering technical standards for systems of music recording and reproduction, it also seeks to influence legislation on copyright and protect the interests of their member labels. The RIAA has been involved in numerous lawsuits against infringers for the downloading of music, as well as actions such as the suit against Rio alleging that its MP3 player in the late 1990s violated the Audio Home Recording Act.

The RIAA is also responsible for certifying album sales as gold (500,000 units), platinum (1,000,000 units), and diamond (10,000,000 units). Other awards are available for certain levels of single and digital sales.

The alleged failure of the recording industry to proactively respond to the development of new technologies, and its aggressive stance in targeting both Web services and individuals, can be credited with causing a social response that presumes piracy to be acceptable. The public, much of which in the past felt that CD prices were too high, saw record companies suing grandmothers and children for downloading music, which resulted in a public relations nightmare for the record labels. As a result, many consumers responded by believing piracy was okay because labels were the "big corporate enemy." As a result, the new generation of today's music consumers—even some musicians who actually stand to lose income from online piracy—has been indifferent to the labels' woes.

As new technologies emerged, the recording industry fell far behind in implementing new offerings that could provide music to consumers via new formats and monetize their intellectual property assets. While technology and device companies continued the development of new devices to download, store, and transport music, labels spent a large part of their efforts on litigation and trying to maintain old business models. In the fall of 2001, Apple Computer released its first iPod, a music player capable of storing five gigabytes of data, or roughly one thousand songs in MP3 format. Early adopters of the iPod realized they now had a device enabling the easy portability of digital music, including music in a digital format "ripped" from compact discs, and digital music grew quickly as a distribution format. Unfortunately for record labels, those gains came primarily as pirated material traded on peer-to-peer networks. By 2003, record labels and copyright owners realized that digital music had reached a critical mass, despite their resistance to the format and the lack of a viable option for online music sales.

As they found themselves behind the times and figurative eight ball, record company executives finally listened and acquiesced when Steve Jobs, CEO of Apple, approached them about a paid download store, where consumers could purchase single tracks of music that could be transferred to the iPod and played on up to five computers, with their playback limited by means of Apple's FairPlay digital rights management (DRM) technology. Apple rolled out the iTunes Music Store in April of 2003, a full four years after Napster's introduction, and initially offered over 200,000 tracks from the five major record labels. The rapid adoption of the digital delivery of music, which happened almost completely without the permission and/or backing of music labels, had essentially forced record label executives to license their music to Apple for sale under a paid download scheme, since the alternative was the continued loss of revenue to digital piracy.

WHAT IS "DRM"?

DRM, or digital rights management, is a mechanism included in files to, among other things, ensure that the files cannot be shared beyond the initial permissions granted by the provider of the file. In Apple's case with FairPlay, a song could only be authorized to play on five computers. Attempts to play the song on additional computers would require a user to enter a password to access the file. Separately, Microsoft's Janus DRM system enables systems such as Rhapsody's tethered downloads for subscriptions, by requiring the player to be plugged in monthly to confirm a subscription is valid. If a user has cancelled his or her subscription, Janus will disable the downloaded files.

While DRM played a significant role in getting the record labels to sell their catalogs on the iTunes store, Apple and most other large online music retailers have now made music available for purchase without built-in playback or copying protection or other restriction mechanisms. Many in the industry saw it as Apple's attempt to head off a United States legal battle on Apple's failure to make the iPod and iTunes store operable with other systems or to license its FairPlay DRM system. (Apple has already faced legislative and legal action across Europe due to its lack of interoperability.) Others have seen it as a response to Amazon's offering of DRM-free files. So instead of opening Apple's proprietary platform, Jobs worked with the record labels to effectively open their DRM protected proprietary works to legal distribution without copy protection. Apple also continues to forego a subscription model that is compatible with the iPod, despite some cries from executives and researchers that a subscription-based service might increase music-based revenue to above that of the late 1990s, before the industry was struck by Napster and the ensuing widespread piracy.

WHY IS COPYRIGHT IMPORTANT TO MUSIC?

The foregoing brief history of the music business illustrates the importance of copyright law to the music industry. Copyright is the right of its owner (typically the creator) to control various uses and distributions of his or her creations. It is copyright that protects music created and the creator's right to make money from such music, and *without it, there would be no recorded music industry.*

Copyright was initially conceived to protect authors and developers of creative works from having their works stolen and to provide them with a source of revenue, which would hopefully spur creativity. Modern copyright law has its origins in British stationers' attempts to protect works from piracy through the passage of the Statute of Anne in 1710, which gave the monopoly control over a work back to the author instead of a publisher. In an effort to encourage creativity, the United States Congress enacted the first copyright legislation in the United States in 1790 to provide a mechanism for protection and reward for authors and creators of artistic works. This first law protected maps, charts, and books for a period of fourteen years, with fourteen-year renewals.

Copyright law was expanded in 1909, offering protection to and extending the life of the term of copyright to twenty-eight years, with twenty-eight year renewals. The 1909 Act also expanded the list of protected works, and for the first time, introduced the concept of a compulsory license for musical works, which is a key part of the foundation of today's music industry. However, sound recordings did not officially qualify for copyright protection under federal law until 1971; they had previously been protected, if at all, under state law.

In 1976, Congress completely rewrote the United States Copyright Act, and that law forms the basis for authors, musicians, and other creators to derive income from their works today.

Anno Octavo

Annæ Reginæ.

An Act for the Encouragement of Learning, by Vesting the Copies of Printed Books in the Authors or Purchasers of such Copies, during the Times therein mentioned.

Hereas Printers, Booksellers, and other Persons have of late frequently taken the Liberty of Printing, Reprinting, and Publishing, or causing to be Printed, Reprinted, and Published Books, and other Writings, without the Consent of the Authors or Proprietors of such Books and Writings, to their very great Detriment, and too often to the Ruin of them and their Families: For Preventing therefore such Practices for the future, and for the Encouragement of Learned Men to Compose and Write useful Books; May it please Your Majesty, that it may be Enacted, and be it Enacted by the Queens most Excellent Majesty, by and with the Advice and Consent of the Lords Spiritual and Temporal, and Commons in this present Parliament Assembled, and by the Authority of the same, That from and after the Tenth Day of April, One thousand seven hundred and ten, the Author of any Book or Books already Printed, who hath not Transferred to any other the Copy or Copies of such Book or Books, Share or Shares thereof, or the Bookseller or Booksellers, Printer or Printers, or other Person or Persons, who hath or have Purchased or Acquired the Copy or Copies of any Book or Books, in order to Print or Reprint the same, shall have the sole Right and Liberty of Printing such Book and Books for the Term of One and twenty Years, to Commence from the said Tenth Day of April, and no longer; and that the Author of any Book or Books already Composed and not Printed and Published, or that shall hereafter be Composed, and his Assignee, or Assigns, shall have the sole Liberty of Printing and Reprinting such Book and Books for the Term of Four-

6   Ttt 2   teen

Fig. 1.4. The Statute of Anne

CHAPTER 2

Current Copyright Basics

The development of copyright law has been largely reactive; it has evolved from its earlier renditions in response to changing industry and intellectual property rights demands. The law can be traced back to Congress's power in the Constitution "to promote the Progress of Science and useful Arts, by securing for limited times to Authors and Inventors the exclusive Right to their Writings and Discoveries."[1] For example, as mentioned earlier, the development of radio brought concern to copyright owners that the provision of free music would provide them no gain and instead diminish the value of their intellectual property. However, unlike the technologies of today, copyright owners found that then existing copyright law already protected their rights, and the new technology led to the development of new methods for collecting revenue.

TWO COPYRIGHTS

There are *two* copyrights vital to the music business, protecting every recorded song:

1. The copyright in the *musical composition* (song)—the lyrics and music; and
2. The copyright in the *sound recording*—the actual recorded performance of a particular musical composition.

---

1 *United States Constitution*, Article 1, Section 8

Artistic works in the United States today are protected under the Copyright Act of 1976, with various amendments. Specifically, the law protects:

> ...works of authorship fixed in any tangible medium of expression, now known or later developed, from which they can be perceived, reproduced, or otherwise communicated, either directly or with the aid of a machine or device...

—Copyright Act of 1976, 17 U.S.C § 102

This means that a work must be written down, recorded, or somehow preserved outside the brain of its creator in order for copyright protection to apply. This was a change from earlier laws that required actual publication of the work for the copyright to *vest*—to become legally yours.

The Copyright Act lists eight categories of works to be covered, although the list is not meant to be all encompassing:

1. literary works;
2. musical works, including any accompanying words;
3. dramatic works, including any accompanying music;
4. pantomimes and choreographic works;
5. pictorial, graphic, and sculptural works;
6. motion pictures and other audiovisual works;
7. sound recordings; and
8. architectural works.

—Copyright Act of 1976, 17 U.S.C § 102

We must note that copyright *does not* protect ideas or concepts, but rather the *expressions* of ideas or concepts. For example, copyright law protects the layout of a version of the yellow pages, but not the phone numbers and addresses included. Specific to music, Bob Dylan's lyrics and melody to "Hurricane" are covered, while the idea of a wrongly imprisoned man is not.

COPYRIGHT'S SIX EXCLUSIVE RIGHTS

1. Reproduction
2. The preparation of derivative works
3. Distribution
4. Public performance
5. Public display
6. Public performance of a sound recording in non-exempt digital formats

Copyright law in the United States provides a copyright owner of a protected work with six exclusive rights in that work:

- *To reproduce the copyrighted work in copies or phonorecords;*
- *To prepare derivative works based upon the copyrighted work;*
- *To distribute copies or phonorecords of the copyrighted work to the public by sale or other transfer of ownership, or by rental, lease, or lending;*
- *In the case of literary, musical, dramatic, and choreographic works, pantomimes, and motion pictures and other audiovisual works, to perform the copyrighted work publicly;*
- *In the case of literary, musical, dramatic, and choreographic works, pantomimes, and pictorial, graphic, or sculptural works, including the individual images of a motion picture or other audiovisual work, to display the copyrighted work publicly; and*
- *In the case of sound recordings, to perform the copyrighted work publicly by means of a digital audio transmission.*

—Copyright Act of 1976, 17 U.S.C § 106

The first of these rights, the right to reproduce the work, means that copyright owners can control the copying of their works. They have the exclusive right to make copies, or to prevent others from copying their works. This could encompass everything from the duplication of an album or sheet music to the use of a song lyric in another musical work.

The second exclusive right, the right to prepare derivative works, is similar to the right to prevent copies from being made. In this case, a copyright owner can prevent all others from making derivative works that are based on the original work (or "loose copies" of the original work). Copyright law defines a derivative work as follows:

> ...a work based upon one or more preexisting works, such as a translation, musical arrangement, dramatization, fictionalization, motion picture version, sound recording, art reproduction, abridgment, condensation, or any other form in which a work may be recast, transformed, or adapted. A work consisting of editorial revisions, annotations, elaborations, or other modifications which, as a whole, represent an original work of authorship, is a "derivative work."

—Copyright Act of 1976, 17 U.S.C § 101

CAN YOU BORROW A RIFF?

A young guitarist loves Slash and the Guns N' Roses song "Sweet Child O' Mine." He "borrows" the main riff from the song and the chorus, and includes them in a new song he writes.

Can he legally do this?

Answer: *No. Guns N' Roses, as the writer of the song (or their assignee), controls the right to prevent others from using part of their song to create another work. Not only does copyright law allow Guns N' Roses to prevent copying of their work, the young guitarist's song could be considered a derivative work under copyright law, and Guns N' Roses has the right to control such adaptations of their work.*

The third right, "to distribute copies or phonorecords of the copyrighted work," reserves the right of distribution to a copyright holder—the creator of the music—unless he or she transfers that right to someone else. The restriction takes the exclusive right to copy to a different level, meaning a band can authorize unlimited copies of their most recent single to be pressed, but can still control where and how those copies are provided to the public. For example, they may choose not to allow online distribution of their single. This exclusive right becomes increasingly important as distribution methods evolve, and we'll discuss it more later in the book as we move into our analysis of online delivery of music.

PERFORMANCE RIGHTS ORGANIZATIONS

Collecting societies exist in most developed countries. In the U.S., ASCAP, BMI, and SESAC compete to sign writers (see appendix B for contact information). In most other countries, a single, government-controlled collecting society exists to collect public performance royalties for copyright holders. Interestingly enough, in nearly every other developed country, sound recording copyright holders are also eligible to exercise public performance rights in their copyrights and receive income from analog transmissions of their works (such as traditional AM and FM radio).

Some foreign societies include:

- France: Société des auteurs, compositeurs et éditeurs de musique
  <www.sacem.fr>
- Italy: Società Italiana degli Autori ed Editori
  <www.siae.it>
- Japan: Japanese Society for Rights of Authors, Composers and Publishers
- Spain: Sociedad General de Autores y Editores
  <www.sgae.es>
- The Netherlands: Buma/Stemra
  <www.bumastemra.nl>
- UK: Performing Right Society (PRS), now known as PRS For Music:
  <www.prsformusic.com

The fourth right, "to publicly perform" a work, is of special concern in the music industry. The right essentially permits a copyright holder to control public performances of a creative work. Such "public performances" include the "performance" of a composition via an on-demand stream rendered over the Internet. The right does not extend to sound recordings (an exception is made for digital performances, which we address in a moment), but covers musical composition copyrights. (This means that artists are not paid when their song is played on the radio, but writers/musical compositions copyright holders are.) It is the public performance right that led to the development of performing rights organizations (PROs), which are responsible for collecting revenues from television and radio broadcasters and live music venues and then distributing the monies to their member writers and publishers. The PROs for musical works—in the U.S., the American Society of Composers, Authors and Publishers (ASCAP), Broadcast Music, Inc. (BMI), and the Society of European Stage Authors and Composers (SESAC)— pay their writers and publishers based on complicated formulas that track airplay and determine how much the writers (and/or copyrights owners, as the case may be) of a musical composition should be paid for the public performances of their song.

The fifth right, "to publicly display" a work, is not of as much concern for the music industry. It is, however, an important right for visual artists such as painters. For musicians, from a logistical perspective, the right applies only to musical works because "sound recordings" cannot by their nature be displayed. An inference can be drawn that the only protection, therefore, for music under this right is the right to control the public exhibition of lyrics and music notes to a musical work. Music is generally protected by the right to publicly perform a work, as discussed above.

The sixth right, "of public performance for sound recordings in digital transmissions," was added to copyright law by Congress with the passage of the Digital Performance Right in Sound Recordings Act of 1995 (the DPRSRA). (We will discuss the history of DPRSRA and its ramifications in more detail in chapter 3.) As we mentioned earlier, sound recordings do not currently fall under the fourth exclusive right of copyright holders (public performance), although musical compositions do. Again, this means that artists or record labels or whoever controls the copyright in a sound recording (the "recorded performance" of a certain song) do not receive public performance income for airplay on terrestrial radio. However, with the passage of the DPRSRA, copyright owners of sound recordings have the right to collect royalties for the public performance of their works through digital means. Digital radio or "webcasting" licenses are granted pursuant to a compulsory license administered by a government-sanctioned arm of the RIAA, SoundExchange. On-demand streaming licenses are voluntary and are negotiated with each sound recording copyright holder individually.

WHO PAYS RADIO ROYALTIES?

A band, Wanton Success, records an original song and releases it as a single to terrestrial radio, satellite radio, and digital radio stations who stream the song to online listeners. From whom should Wanton Success expect to receive public performance royalty payments for the song?

Answer: *Satellite radio will be required to compensate Wanton Success for airplay of their song as both the writers and the performers. Terrestrial radio will not be required to pay for the public performance of the* **sound recording** *but will be required to pay public performance royalties to the band as the writers of the* **composition***. Any terrestrial radio station that also streams their station online (or any other online broadcaster) will also be required to make royalty payments to the band for the public performance of the sound recording via streaming to SoundExchange and the musical composition to one of the PROs.*

TRANSFERRING COPYRIGHT

Any of the six exclusive rights of a copyright owner, or all of them together, may be given or sold to a third party. Four types of transfers exist for copyrighted works:

- Assignment
- Exclusive License
- Non-exclusive License
- Work for Hire

A copyright owner may grant his or her rights in a work to a third party (i.e., give those rights away) for either a specified period of time (license) or in perpetuity (assignment).[2] (Such a transfer must be in writing and signed by the owner of the rights conveyed.) For example, in a publishing deal, a songwriter may assign all or part of the copyright in his or her song to a publisher in exchange for an advance of royalties and the opportunity to have the publisher place the song on other artists' albums or in film and television. Separately, an artist might license his or her sound recordings to a record label for a period of time, during which the label will try to profit from distributing the recordings.

Under a *license*, the licensee's right to the copyright will terminate upon expiration of the license term, returning the rights to the copyright owner. Under an *assignment*, the acquirer of the rights maintains the rights until the copyright expires, with one caveat: Under U.S. copyright law, an assignor of rights is entitled to terminate the assignment during the five year period beginning in the 35th year after the transfer of right.[3] (The period is during the five years after the first fifty-six years, or January 1, 1978, whichever comes first, for works created before January 1, 1978.) So, in the example above, the songwriter could terminate the assignment of his or her copyright to the publisher after thirty-five years and regain ownership of the song. Recent court cases have held that this right to a termination of transfer cannot be waived contractually in the initial sale agreement.

Finally, there also exists in copyright law the concept of a *work for hire*. A work for hire is a creative work that is deemed to have been commissioned specially by an employer, and the employer will own the copyright from the work's inception (as opposed to the case of an assignment, in which case the copyright is deemed to have vested in the creator upon creation, and the rights are later assigned or given to someone else). There need not be, however, an employer-employee relationship between the creator and the person commissioning the work for hire; a contract stipulating that the work is to be a work for hire upon its inception will suffice.

The Copyright Act specifically defines "work for hire" as:

(1) a work prepared by an employee within the scope of his or her employment, or

---

2 *Copyright Act of 1976, 17 U.S.C § 201(d)*
3 *Copyright Act of 1976, 17 U.S.C § 203(a)(3)*

(2) a work specially ordered or commissioned for use as a contribution to a collective work, as a part of a motion picture or other audiovisual work, as a sound recording, as a translation, as a supplementary work, as a compilation, as an instructional text, as a test, as answer material for a test, or as an atlas, if the parties expressly agree in a written instrument signed by them that the work shall be considered a work made for hire.

—*Copyright Act of 1976, 17 U.S.C § 101*

Because the copyright vests in someone other than the creator at the moment the work is created, there is no right to termination of transfer. The distinction becomes important as we talk about recording agreements. A recording agreement that states that the creator will assign the works (i.e., master recording) to a music company will allow the creator to regain copyright ownership in those works after thirty-five years, whereas an artist whose master recording is deemed a work for hire will never regain those rights, because he or she never had them to start. Many film scores are written as works for hire so that the movie studio does not have to worry about a reversion of the copyright interest in the song.

RECLAIMING RIGHTS DUE TO A TRANSFER OF AGREEMENT

Wanton Success signs a recording agreement with XYZ Records, under which the band will assign the rights in their already complete *Album One* to XYZ and will record a new *Album Two* as a work for hire.

Thirty-five years later, the band hears that they can "get their masters back" by notifying the label under the Termination of Transfer provision. Will they be entitled to all of their master recordings?

Answer: *No. The band would be entitled to terminate their assignment of rights in* Album One, *but because* Album Two *was a "work for hire," the copyright vested in XYZ and is not subject to the Termination of Transfer provision.*

FILING AND DEPOSIT REQUIREMENTS

Many people believe that a work must be registered in order to be
protected under U.S. copyright law. Copyright law does require that
all copyrighted works be deposited with the Library of Congress
within three months of publication; ironically, this "requirement"
is not a condition of copyright protection.

Separately, the Register of Copyrights offers an optional registration for copyrights, allowing a copyright holder to place a copy on
file to provide *prima facie* evidence of copyright ownership.[4] (*Prima
facie* evidence is evidence that, unless rebutted, is sufficient to prove
a fact.) This means that a court will weigh the copyright registration
as proof of ownership in any infringement action unless someone
proves otherwise, and the date of registration can be used as proof
of the date of creation. As with the deposit requirement for the
Library of Congress, registration is not required for copyright to vest.

HOW TO REGISTER A COPYRIGHT

Forms for registration can be found at www.copyright.gov, and
online filing is available. Form CO can be used to file for both the
sound recording and musical composition copyright, although
separate forms must be filled out for each copyright. Deposit
with the Library of Congress is sufficient to fulfill the deposit
requirements of the Copyright Office, but the registration forms and
fees must still be paid. Current fees are $35 for online registration
and $50 for paper registration.

Remember, copyright always vests in a created work at the time
of creation, in either the creator or the employer or other assignee.
Registration is a prerequisite to the filing of lawsuit for infringement.

Rather than filing for a copyright registration, some people
choose to use what is commonly referred to as the "poor man's
copyright." By mailing a copy of a work to yourself, having the post
office postmark the envelope, and then not opening the envelope,

---

4 *Copyright Act of 1976, 17 U.S.C § 407*

you may be able to show a date of creation of the work, which took place prior to the postmark. While it's better than nothing, it is certainly not as effective as a formal copyright registration.

The main point here is that having evidence to prove the date of creation, whether in the form of official registration, publication and distribution, witness testimony, or other proof, will help prove your case in an infringement action.

SHOULD I COPYRIGHT MY WORK?

Many artists often wonder if they should bother to "copyright" their work. However, copyright vests in their work the minute it is fixed to a medium. Most often, they are referring to the registration process, which is optional. *Registration is only required if you want to sue someone else for copyright infringement. It does not affect whether you hold the rights in your work.*

HOW DO I REGISTER THE COPYRIGHT IN MY WORK?

Wanton Success has finished their first full-length studio album, which consists of twelve songs they fully wrote. They want to register their copyrights in both the sound recordings and musical compositions. Can they file just one copyright registration form, or will they need to register each song individually?

Answer: *Wanton Success will have to register the musical composition copyrights individually for each musical composition, at a charge of $35 per song. They can register the copyright in the sound recordings through one fee of $35 for all sound recordings encompassed on the album. (The $35 fee is for online filings as of 2009.)*

NOTICE

Notice is also no longer a requirement for copyright in the United States, meaning that copyright owners are not required to put any type of notification on copies of their work. Of course, you are always free to include it anyway, and we suggest including it on any mass-distributed copies, showing the year of creation and the owner.

APPROPRIATE NOTICE FORMATS

Copyright notice is not required, but the appropriate format, if you do choose to include it on copies of your work, is © for visually perceptible works, along with the year of first publication of the work and the name of the copyright owner, and   for sound recordings such as phonorecords, also along with the year of first publication of the work and the name of the copyright owner. As an example, this book is © Berklee Press, 2009.

The phrase "All Rights Reserved" can also be used, but does not hold much weight in the United States. Prior to 2000, the phrase was required by countries who were signatories to the Buenos Aires Convention (see chapter 11), but the requirement no longer exists. Today, it may help reserve what are called "moral rights" in some foreign countries ("moral rights" are not recognized in the U.S.), which generally provide a right of attribution to the work and the right to protect the "integrity of the work."

DURATION OF COPYRIGHT

Copyright has a limited duration during which the owner can exercise his or her exclusive rights. Any works created after January 1, 1978 are protected for a period of the life of the creator plus 70 years. This means that if you create a work, copyright will last throughout your lifetime and your heirs or other owners of the copyright will be entitled to enforce the copyright in the work for 70 years from the date of your death. Anonymous works (or works created under a pseudonym) and works for hire have protection for 95 years from the date of first publication, or 120 years from the date of creation, whichever expires first.[5]

---

5 *Copyright Act of 1976, 17 U.S.C § 302*

LENGTH OF COPYRIGHT PROTECTION

Date of Creation	Copyright Term
Prior to January 1, 1978 but not expiring before December 31, 2002	28 years + 67 year renewal term
Prior to January 1, 1978 but set to expire before December 31, 2002	Will not expire before 12/31/2047
After January 1, 1978	Life of the author + 70 years

Copyright duration becomes more complicated for those works created before January 1, 1978. Any work created prior to January 1, 1978 in which copyright would not have expired before December 31, 2002, is entitled to an initial term of protection of 28 years, with the right of renewal for an additional 67 years. Works created prior to January 1, 1978 but which would have expired before December 31, 2002 now will continue to have copyright protection until at least December 31, 2047. (The Sonny Bono Copyright Extension Act, passed in 1998, extended the term of copyright by 20 years. The Act was widely known as the "Mickey Mouse Extension Act," as it was fought for by entertainment companies who didn't want to lose protection for their older assets and effectively granted Disney additional protection for the Mickey Mouse character.)

COPYRIGHT DURATION OF WORKS FOR HIRE

Works for hire are protected for a different period of time than works in which copyright vests in the original author. Protection lasts for 95 years from the date of first publication, or 120 years from the date of creation, whichever comes first.

When copyright protection ends for a creative work, it is said to have fallen into the "public domain." A work in the public domain may be used by any person for any purpose, including the creation of derivative works, without restriction or payment to the original author. Many old church hymns, the national anthem, and older "campfire songs" all became public domain many years ago. Further, new arrangements of public domain works (e.g., adding lyrics to a Beethoven piano concerto) are subject to new copyright protection with the same rights and protections as works not created from public domain source material.

ENFORCING COPYRIGHTS

If someone infringes one or more of a copyright holder's exclusive rights—for example, by plagiarizing a song's lyrics or melody—copyright law has established a series of remedies available to the copyright owner if he or she sues and prevails in a court of law. Those remedies include:

Injunctive relief.[6] Injunctive relief means that a court of law could issue a ruling to stop the infringement immediately, whether or not a trial is pending regarding the infringement. An injunction might prohibit the manufacture and sale of an item that is alleged to infringe upon the rights of a valid copyright holder. For example, a CD containing a song that is alleged to have copied lyrics from a prior musical work could be removed from store shelves under a court order. RealNetworks was granted an injunction against Streambox in 1999 stopping Streambox from distributing products that violated the DMCA, and the original Napster was essentially forced out of business by a 2001 injunction requiring the company to filter copyrighted material (because they didn't have the technology in place to do so).

Impounding of infringing items.[7] A court could also issue an order requiring police to impound all items that are infringing. Upon final judgment that the items do infringe the rights of a third party, the court also has the authority to order destruction of the infringing property. For example, New York City Police could raid a warehouse containing illegal copies of compact discs and impound them until a trial adjudicates the matter. In 2005, the Sixth Circuit court ordered all copies of the first album by Notorious B.I.G., entitled *Ready to Die*, impounded after the

---

6 *Copyright Act of 1976, 17 U.S.C § 502*
7 *Copyright Act of 1976, 17 U.S.C § 503*

court found that the album contained an unlicensed sample of the Ohio Players 1972 song "Singing in the Morning."[8] Note that this remedy could not physically apply to items copied in cyberspace or digital piracy, because those items by their non-physical nature cannot be impounded.

Actual damages, plus profits made by the infringer from the infringing works.[9] If an item is deemed to be infringing, a copyright holder is entitled to recover the actual damages suffered by him or her as a result of the infringement. He or she is also entitled to any profits of the infringer that are not taken into account as part of the actual damages. In the Notorious B.I.G case, the plaintiffs were awarded $733,378 in "compensatory damages" related to the profits from the infringing material.[10]

Statutory damages.[11] Copyright law also sets forth certain minimum damages that can be awarded to a copyright holder from an infringer (known as *statutory damages*). The copyright owner may elect prior to final judgment to receive an award of statutory damages in lieu of actual damages, which amount for all infringements in the action shall be at least $750 but less than $30,000. If a copyright is deemed to have been infringed willfully, the amount can be up to $150,000 per work infringed, but if the court finds the infringer was not aware and had no reason to be aware of his or her infringement, the statutory damages may be reduced to as low as $200 per work. Again, in the Notorious B.I.G. case, the plaintiffs also received an award of $150,000, the statutory maximum.[12]

Criminal penalties. If the infringement was committed willfully for purposes of commercial gain, or by the reproduction of one or more copies of a phonorecord or other copyrighted work within a 180-day period, or by making a work available to the public via a computer network, the infringer may be punished under criminal penalties set forth in 18 U.S.C. §2319. Several members of the aPOCALYPSE pRODUCTION cREW warez group online were

---

8 Bridgeport Music, Inc. v. Justin Combs Publishing, 507 F.3d 470

9 *Copyright Act of 1976, 17 U.S.C § 504*

10 Bridgeport Music, Inc. v. Justin Combs Publishing, 507 F.3d 470

11 *Copyright Act of 1976, 17 U.S.C § 504*

12 Bridgeport Music, Inc. v. Justin Combs Publishing, 507 F.3d 470

sent to prison for criminal copyright infringement for operating a service online for the illicit sharing of music on private servers. (Although not in the U.S., and therefore not under U.S. law, founders of the offshore file sharing service the Pirate Bay were also sent to jail in Sweden for criminal copyright infringement.) Criminal penalties can include:

- Making copies of a copyrighted work for financial gain: A minimum of 1 year in jail, and the penalties are stepped up to five years if the total value exceeded $2,500.
- Making copies of copyright work, including via electronic means: A penalty of a year, or three years if the offense includes works that have a total retail value of $2,500 or more.
- Making a copyrighted work available on a computer network: Up to three years in prison, or up to five years if such actions were for commercial advantage or financial gain.
- Specific to music: Anyone who records a live performance, or transmits or distributes such a live music performance, can be punished by up to a five-year jail penalty for the first offense.

Infringement actions must, by law, be instituted within three years after a claim arose for civil penalties or within five years after a criminal cause of action arose.

WHAT SHOULD I DO IF I THINK SOMEONE IS INFRINGING MY COPYRIGHT?

Wanton Success wrote a song five years ago, and now a band called the Copier has released a song that contains my exact lyrics, but they credit themselves with writing it. What should the band do to protect its rights?

Answer: *If Wanton Success believes someone has copied its work, or is otherwise infringing on its copyright, there are several steps it should take:*

Consider sending a "cease and desist letter." Such a letter informs or reminds the other party of the band's rights. A cease and desist letter typically demands removal of the infringing content from the market, and an accounting (detailed record of all sales or distributions) and fees for such uses (occasionally including attorneys fees as well). Such a letter can also demand a license in the event that you just want to start collecting royalties for the use. This is generally the first step an attorney will take.

If the cease and desist letter doesn't work, the band will probably have to file a lawsuit against the other party in federal district court, setting forth its claims and the damages the band is seeking. In Wanton Success's case, there are certain tests created by courts that must be passed to prove the Copier copied its song, including substantial similarity of the works, and that the Copier had access to its work. (Usually a musicologist is hired as an expert witness to testify about the similar nature of the material). Also, remember that Wanton Success must file within three years of the Copier's release for a civil claim or five years for a criminal action.

As always in a case like this, it's best for the band to consult an attorney to ensure its rights are properly protected.

DEFENSES AVAILABLE IN INFRINGEMENT ACTIONS

The copying or sale of a copy of a copyrighted work is not always considered to be infringement. Congress has created exclusions to copyright, which will permit the use of a protected work in certain situations.

The Fair Use Defense

Perhaps the most prominent defense to copyright infringement is the *fair use* defense, which relates to certain uses of creative works that are deemed important to the advancement of society as a whole. Use for educational purposes, news reporting, research, and criticism are all examples of what may fall under the fair use doctrine.

The Copyright Act sets forth a four-prong test, which is applied in determining if a defendant's use qualifies as a permitted fair use:

- *The purpose and character of the use, including whether such use is of a commercial nature or is for nonprofit educational purposes;*
- *The nature of the copyrighted work;*
- *The amount and substantiality of the portion used in relation to the copyrighted work as a whole;*
- *The effect of the use upon the potential market for or value of the copyrighted work.*

—*Copyright Act of 1976, 17 U.S.C § 107*

According to the Copyright Office, the 1961 Report of the Register of Copyrights on the General Revision of the U.S. Copyright Law cites examples of activities that courts have regarded as fair use, including:

quotation of excerpts in a review or criticism for purposes of illustration or comment; quotation of short passages in a scholarly or technical work, for illustration or clarification of the author's observations; use in a parody of some of the content of the work parodied; summary of an address or article, with brief quotations, in a news report; reproduction by a library of a portion of a work to replace part of a damaged copy; reproduction by a teacher or student of a small part of a work to illustrate a lesson; reproduction of a work in legislative or judicial proceedings or reports; incidental and fortuitous reproduction, in a newsreel or broadcast, of a work located in the scene of an event being reported.

—www.copyright.gov

A SAMPLE ANALYSIS: CAMPBELL AKA LUKE SKYYWALKER V. ACUFF-ROSE MUSIC, INC., SUPREME COURT OF THE UNITED STATES, 510 US 569

In 1994, in a landmark case analysis of the fair use doctrine, the Supreme Court held that 2 Live Crew and their record label, Luke Skyywalker Records, did not infringe the rights of Acuff-Rose Publishing when they wrote a parody version of Roy Orbison's song "Pretty Woman." (Orbison and his co-writer had assigned their rights to Acuff-Rose Music, Inc. in 1964.)

In 1989, Luther Campbell, a member of 2 Live Crew, wrote a song called "Pretty Woman," he testified, "through comical lyrics, to satirize the original work." The band asked Acuff-Rose for permission to use the song, and offered to credit Acuff-Rose as the owner of the song, as well as to pay a fee for the use. Acuff-Rose refused to grant permission, and the band released the song anyway.

The next year, after nearly 250,000 copies of the song had been sold, Acuff-Rose sued 2 Live Crew and Luke Skyywalker Records, and the district court granted summary judgment for 2 Live Crew. The court viewed 2 Live Crew's song as a parody, and established that despite the band's commercial gain from the song, the band was protected by the fair use defense. The Court of Appeals for the Sixth Circuit reversed the decision, concluding that the song's "blatantly commercial purpose prevents this parody from being a fair use."

The Supreme Court, in its analysis, offered a historical perspective on the purpose of the fair use doctrine:

> From the infancy of copyright protection, some opportunity for fair use of copyrighted materials has been thought necessary to fulfill copyright's very purpose, "to promote the Progress of Science and useful Arts. . . ." U.S. Const., Art I, §8, cl.8. For as Justice Story explained, "in truth, in literature, in science and in art, there are, and can be, few, if any, things, which in an abstract sense, are strictly new and original throughout. Every book in literature, science and art, borrows, and must necessarily borrow, and use much which was well known and used before."
>
> —Emerson v. Davies, 8 F. Cas 615, 619 (No.4, 436)
>
> (C.C.D. Mass 1845) . . .

. . . Congress meant §107 to restate the present judicial doctrine of fair use, not to change, narrow, or enlarge it in any way and intended that courts continue the common law tradition of fair use adjudication. The fair use doctrine thus "permits [and requires] courts to avoid rigid application of the copyright statute when, on occasion, it would stifle the very creativity which that law is designed to foster."

—*Stewart v. Abend, 495 US 207, 236 (1990)*[13]

The court went on to analyze 2 Live Crew's version of the song through the four-prong test for fair use. Under the first prong, the court noted that "transformative" works may lessen the significance of other factors such as commercialism. The court found that parodies can provide social benefit, and are entitled to present a legitimate fair use defense. Their opinion noted that merely because a work was used for commercial purposes did not necessarily preclude a fair use defense, for news reporting, research, teaching, and education are "generally conducted for a profit" in this country.

The second factor, according to the court, was satisfied. Parodies by their nature copy "publicly known, expressive works."

When analyzing the third factor, "the amount and substantiality of the portion used in relation to the copyrighted work as a whole," the court found that a parody must sometimes use the "heart" of a work in order to conjure up the original in order for listeners to correctly make the object of the parody recognizable. Despite the fact that 2 Live Crew copied the signature bass riff of the original "Pretty Woman," they had added "distinctive sounds," interposing "scraper" noise, overlaying the music with solos in different keys, and altering the drum beat. It found that the parody itself had added enough substantial elements, when compared to the original, to offset the fact that 2 Live Crew had taken the "heart" of the song.

Finally, the court drew a correlation to a "scathing theater review" when scrutinizing the song under the fourth lens of the test, "the effect of the use upon the potential market for or value of the copyrighted work" and noted that a court must distinguish between "biting criticism [that merely] suppresses demand and copyright infringement which usurps it." In other words, a parody typically

---

13   Campbell AKA Luke Skyywalker v. Acuff-Rose Music Inc., Supreme Court of the United States, 510 US 569

does not serve as a substitute for the original, but instead creates its own market. The court also addressed whether or not a parody might have affected the market for a rap derivative work of "Pretty Woman," but that neither side had introduced evidence on this aspect in the trial.

Ultimately, the court decided that 2 Live Crew's version of "Pretty Woman" was a fair one, and upheld the right to create parodies without fear of infringement suits (assuming such parodies manage to pass the four-part test set forth in Section 107 of the Copyright Act).

(*The court, in a rare show of humor, explicitly stated that they would not evaluate the quality of a parody, and that "whether, going beyond that, parody is in good taste or bad does not and should not matter to fair use."*)

Original:

Pretty woman, walking down the street,

Pretty Woman, the kind I like to meet,

Pretty Woman, I don't believe you,

You're not the truth,

No one could look as good as you Mercy"

2 Live Crew:

Pretty woman, walkin' down the street,

Pretty woman, girl you look so sweet,

Pretty woman, you bring me down to that knee,

Pretty woman, you make me wanna beg please,

Oh pretty woman"

In recorded music, the fair use defense is commonly used to defend parodies (think Weird Al Yankovic) and the use of certain portions. There is, however, a fine line between fair use and the need for a sampling license. We'll discuss sampling (the use of one song within another) in a bit.

Copyright also provides a defense for those who wish to sell their individual copy of a particular work. Under the *first sale* doctrine, a creator should only profit from the first sale of his or her original work (or a particular copy). The Copyright Act states:

. . . the owner of a particular copy or phonorecord lawfully made under this title, or any person

authorized by such owner, is entitled, without the authority of the copyright owner, to sell or otherwise dispose of the possession of that copy or phonorecord.

—*Copyright Act of 1976, 17 U.S.C § 109(a)*

This means that despite the efforts of artists such as Garth Brooks, who decried CD resale shops in the late 1990s for reducing revenue streams to artists and songwriters, owners of a particular copy may sell their copy of a particular work to whomever they choose, without penalty. Garth Brooks refused to ship his CD *In Pieces* to stores dealing in used CDs until his actions were shut down as the result of an anti-trust lawsuit against his label, Capitol Records.

SELLING USED STUFF

If copyright protects a creator's ability to manufacture and distribute copies of his or her work, why can I sell my used Rolling Stone CDs or my Van Gogh print?

Answer: *The first sale doctrine allows owners of a particular copy of a work to sell that particular copy of the work. In essence, a copyright holder is by law only entitled to profit from the first sale of each individual copy of his or her work.*

INTERNATIONAL PROTECTION OF COPYRIGHT

American creators and copyright owners may wonder if their works are protected overseas and in foreign countries, since the United States Congress passed the copyright law originally covering their work. To solve this issue, a number of international treaties have been signed to ensure copyright protection of works in other juris-dictions. We'll discuss these treaties in chapter 11 when we discuss international issues.

CHAPTER 3

Copyright in Music

As we saw in chapter 2, today, the music industry is built on two major copyrights:

1. the copyright in the *musical work* (i.e., the song: music and lyrics) and
2. the copyright in the *sound recording* (i.e., the recorded performance, or an artist's interpretation of the song).

Each of these provides the copyright owner of a musical composition or a sound recording with the same exclusive rights granted to all copyright holders under copyright law, with two exceptions: (a) there is no right of public display for a sound recording, due to the very nature of the work; and (b) there is no right of public performance for sound recordings other than in digital transmissions. This distinction between the two copyrights is important, because the rights granted to musical works are more encompassing than those of sound recordings.

There is also a differentiation in how we analyze how copyright owners and administrators (such as record labels and music publishers) monetize their copyright, because different rules apply to each copyright. For example, owners of music publishing copyrights receive a payment for public performances on traditional "over-the-air" radio and television broadcasts, while sound recording copyright holders do not. Incidentally, nearly every country around the world except the United States requires public performance royalties to be paid to sound recording copyright holders for all broadcasts. At the time of press, a revision to the law (via the Performance Rights Act) to bring the U.S. in line with the rest of the world on this issue was being considered.

MUSICAL WORKS SPECIFICS

The exclusive right of public performance for musical works is one of the six rights of a copyright holder, as we saw in chapter 2. Publishing companies, or songwriters, or whoever the copyright holders may be, are entitled to a fee every time their musical work is performed publicly. Examples of public performance range from radio play to live performances to online streaming.

Congress, however, did not initially include a mechanism for musical works rights holders to be paid for public performances. Think of the logistics: thousands of broadcasters, concert halls, restaurants, and other live venues negotiating separately for each song they publicly perform. PROs solve this problem, but PROs were born as a result of litigation. In a case against Bamberger Department Store in Newark, New Jersey in 1922, courts held that the store was broadcasting music throughout its store on a radio station, WOR, and that it was doing so for commercial gain. The performance of the copyrighted song on the radio was therefore a public performance, meaning copyright owners could demand payment for one of their exclusive rights: public performance. The ruling led to the rapid growth of ASCAP, as venues needed a method to clear public performance licenses without going to each publisher. ASCAP today is one of three main PROs in the United States collecting public performance royalties for writers from radio, television, film, and live-venue performances. Each PRO then uses a complicated formula, mostly based on airplay, to determine how much each writer should be paid every accounting period.

The other two PROs in existence today, BMI and SESAC, also developed in the twentieth century. SESAC was formed in 1930 to license European works in the United States. BMI was formed by radio broadcasters as an alternative to ASCAP in 1939, and continues to be owned and operated by major broadcasters today, although it operates as a non-profit. Conversely to ASCAP and BMI, SESAC is the only "for-profit" collecting society. Based in Nashville and owned by private investors, SESAC maintains a strategy of obtaining rights to popular music and using them as leverage in negotiations with broadcasters.

Note that, unlike the competitive atmosphere in the United States, in most countries around the world, a single performing society exists to collect and distribute public performance royalties.

SHOULD I JOIN A PRO?

We are a small independent band, and we write our own material. Our manager advised us to register with a PRO to make more money. What does this mean? Will we actually make money by doing this? Does it cost anything?

Answer: *If you are a writer or owner of the copyright in a song or other musical composition, you should consider joining a PRO if your work might be performed publicly in a broadcast medium such as radio or television, played live at music venues, or streamed online. PROs, which are free to join, generally handle blanket clearance services for the public performance of compositions. Venues (bars, restaurants, retail stores) and services (online services including ad supported and subscription on-demand streaming services) "publicly perform" compositions when they play music for customers. PROs collect negotiated royalty fees from venues and services and distribute them to the appropriate rights holders.*

Your manager is suggesting that you register with a PRO so that you can collect royalties for public performance of your compositions. Again, PROs are free to join. The admission/registration process with any of them is easy and reasonable and should, if managed properly, result in an additional revenue stream for writers. ASCAP, for example, processes hundreds of millions of dollars in royalties for its members annually.

There are differences in each PRO in the U.S. ASCAP and BMI are not-for-profit, while SESAC is a for-profit entity that requires an invitation to join. ASCAP was formed by music creators in 1914, and is 100 percent member-owned, while BMI was founded as a competitor to ASCAP in 1939 by radio executives who wanted to provide rights holders an alternative to ASCAP.

- *Today, ASCAP and BMI are open to all writers. Prospective members need only download a membership from their respective Web sites.*
- *Membership in SESAC is by invitation only.*
- *ASCAP and BMI administer the vast majority of compositions commercially available in the United States.*
- *Each company uses a different formula to compute royalty payments to writers. Writers may only belong to one society at a time.*

For more information on each, visit their Web sites at www.ascap.com, www.bmi.com, and www.sesac.com.

Of additional importance to writers is the ability to license their work for inclusion on a sound recording. This license to reproduce a musical composition is called a *mechanical license*, and copyright holders may negotiate whatever rate they desire with the record label or distributor of sound recordings. However, Congress has provided for what is called a "compulsory mechanical license" for musical works. This means that anyone can make and release his or her own sound recording of a musical work once that work has already been distributed to the public, as long as mechanical royalties are paid at the minimum rate or as negotiated with the musical composition copyright holder. (The minimum rate as of 2009 is 9.1 cents per song per album manufactured or track sold).

> When phonorecords of a nondramatic musical work have been distributed to the public in the United States under the authority of the copyright owner, any other person, including those who make phonorecords or digital phonorecord deliveries, may, by complying with the provisions of this section, obtain a compulsory license only if his or her primary purpose in making phonorecords is to distribute them to the public for private use, including by means of digital phonorecord delivery.

—Copyright Act of 1976, 17 U.S.C § 115(a)(1)

Congress has specifically included "digital phonorecord deliveries" in the compulsory licensing scheme, which means that writers are paid at the same mechanical royalty rate for sales on iTunes or other online download services as they would be for the sale of a compact disc. The Harry Fox Agency (HFA) currently serves as a clearinghouse for mechanical licenses in the United States, representing over 37,000 publishers and offering licensees the ability to procure mechanical licenses from a single source rather than contacting each music publisher individually.

A compulsory license will allow an artist to record a song in their own style, as long as fundamental changes to the song, such as significant lyrical changes, are not made. Also, note that the re-recording of a musical work in a style slightly different than that of the original will not confer the rights of a derivative work onto the new work. This allows artists who "cover" a song to alter its style (within the confines of the law) without running up against the exclusive right of the copyright owner to prepare derivative works. It also means that the cover artist will not have any rights in their version of the musical work, even though they may have altered its style slightly.

> A compulsory license includes the privilege of making a musical arrangement of the work to the extent necessary to conform it to the style or manner of interpretation of the performance involved, but the arrangement shall not change the basic melody or fundamental character of the work, and shall not be subject to protection as a derivative work under this title, except with the express consent of the copyright owner.

—*Copyright Act of 1976, 17 U.S.C § 115(a)(2)*

COVERING SONGS IN A DIFFERENT STYLE

Wanton Success wants to cover Snoop Dogg's "Gin and Juice" as a folk song. Is the band able to record the song in such a different light without permission from Snoop Dogg or the other writers?

Answer: *Yes, as long as the basic melody and character of the work are not changed, and mechanical license payments are made to Snoop Dogg (or the current owner of the copyright in the "Gin and Juice" composition).*

Record labels will frequently ask artists who are also writers of their own material for a "controlled composition" clause in their recording agreement. Labels claim that since they are helping the writer/artist distribute the songs they've written and earn mechanical royalties, the label should be entitled to pay mechanical royalties for the songs controlled by the artist (thus the term "controlled compositions") at a reduced rate. This rate is usually 75 percent of the statutory mechanical rate. Similarly, record labels will frequently impose a cap on the number of compositions that may be "payable" per album (usually ten songs for a single-disc album), fix the payable rate at the established rate at the time of release (sometimes even fixed at time of delivery of masters—meaning that the artist won't get the benefit of any increases to the statutory rate), and even limit the number of royalty bearing minutes per recording. These are all methods employed at a time of great leverage to ensure that the labels' mechanical royalty costs are as low as possible, under the circumstances..

Record labels typically do not directly grant the license for the composition, a right that can only be granted by the music publisher or other holder of that composition right. Record labels typically collect this separate fee, however, with an assurance (typically in the form of a representation or warranty) that they will pass the fee for the composition through to the composition right holder. Current mechanical rates are:

Type of Mechanical License	Compulsory License Rate between 1/1/08 and 12/31/12
Songs downloaded or sold in physical format (less than 5 minutes)	9.1 cents
Songs downloaded or sold in physical format (more than 5 minutes)	1.75 cents per minute
Ringtones	24 cents

Fig. 3.1. Rates for Different Mechanical Licenses

ROYALTIES FOR COVERED SONGS

A songwriter composed an entire album of compositions for the popular sixties band, the Bent. For the next three decades, the songwriter, who maintains copyright ownership, collected dwindling mechanical royalties on a per-song basis from the record label that distributed the album. In 2008, three songs from the original album by the Bent were re-recorded as covers by a pop artist whose album is distributed by a different label. The sales of these cover recordings have been significant. Is the songwriter entitled to mechanical royalties for sales of the covers? Who should the songwriter contact to collect such royalties?

Answer: *Yes, the songwriter is absolutely entitled to mechanical royalties in the amount of 9.1 cents per track. The songwriter should contact the record label distributing the pop artist's album to collect such fees on both a retroactive and going-forward basis.*

In the Copyright Act, Congress provided for a mechanism to appoint "Copyright Royalty Judges" who are responsible for setting and adjusting royalty rates, such as the compulsory mechanical license, as provided for in sections 114, 115, 116, 118, and 119 of the Copyright Act. The Librarian of Congress appoints the three judges, who will serve full-time, and generally the judges are required to calculate the rates to achieve certain objectives:

(A) To maximize the availability of creative works to the public;

(B) To afford the copyright owner a fair return for his or her creative work and the copyright user a fair income under existing economic conditions;

(C) To reflect the relative roles of the copyright owner and the copyright user in the product made available to the public with respect to relative creative contribution, technological contribution, capital investment, cost, risk, and contribution to the opening of new markets for creative expression and media for their communication;

(D) To minimize any disruptive impact on the structure of the industries involved and on generally prevailing industry practices.
—*Copyright Act of 1976, 17 U.S.C § 801 (b)(1)*

SPECIAL PROVISIONS FOR SOUND RECORDINGS

While protections under the Copyright Act have served rights holders well for decades, new technologies, unanticipated at the time the Act was written, have raised questions of how to appropriately protect rights in the digital age, and new legislation is regularly considered to address these concerns. For example, as mentioned earlier, the development of the DAT led to the Audio Home Recording Act of 1992, which placed levies on manufacturers whose products might promote infringement. The DAT was widely cited as the first technology to allow repeated copying without loss of quality, and for that reason, labels and musicians lobbied Congress for an amendment to the Copyright Act.

The Audio Home Recording Act provides for a 2 percent royalty on digital audio recording devices. Devices, however, are so narrowly defined in the bill that it means literally only DAT players. Further, the law requires manufacturers of blank media such as blank CDs to pay a 3 percent royalty on sales. The Copyright Office collects the money and pays it out to musical composition and sound recording copyright holders, as well as to non-featured musicians who are members of the American Federation of Musicians (AFM) or American Federation of Radio and Television Artists (AFTRA) unions, who receive a small share.

The law also required manufacturers of DAT players to include a serial copy management system, preventing the recording of subsequent-generation tapes from the original DAT copy. There is no restriction on copying in analog formats.

The royalty payment due under section 1003 for each digital audio recording device imported into and distributed in the United States, or manufactured and distributed in the United States, shall be 2 percent of the transfer price. Only the first person to manufacture and distribute or import and distribute such device shall be required to pay the royalty with respect to such device.

—*Copyright Act of 1976, 17 U.S.C § 1004(a)(1)*

The royalty payments deposited pursuant to section 1005 shall, in accordance with the procedures specified in section 1007, be distributed to any interested copyright party—(1) whose musical work or sound recording has been—(A) embodied in a digital musical recording or an analog musical recording lawfully made under this title that has been distributed, and (B) distributed in the form of digital musical recordings or analog musical recordings or disseminated to the public in transmissions, during the period to which such payments pertain; and (2) who has filed a claim under Section 1007.

—*Copyright Act of 1976, 17 U.S.C § 1006(a)*

FEES FROM HARDWARE MANUFACTURERS?

We have more recently seen efforts by labels, outside copyright law, to receive royalties on the sale of devices. Some labels in 2006 requested a royalty from Microsoft on the sales of the company's Zune portable music player as part of a licensing arrangement for their catalogs of music. This was the first known attempt to "tax" new hardware since the Audio Home Recording Act of 1992 was passed, and they were reportedly successful in their negotiations.

While Congress responded to DAT technologies with a specific solution, other problems are not always easily resolved. Amendments and new legislation are regularly introduced each year to Congress, with very few surviving past the initial Congressional committee review, and even fewer becoming law. We'll discuss attempts to update the law in chapter 9.

However, more changes affecting sound recordings did ensue when digital transmissions of music became available online in the mid 1990s. Congress passed the DPRSRA, an amendment to the Copyright Act, in 1995, which for the first time established a public performance royalty right for the holders of sound recording copyrights. This means that most publicly available digital transmissions of a sound recording, such as Internet radio and satellite radio, now require a royalty payment to the recording's owner. The main exception is a digital transmission of a non-subscription broadcast program, such as digital over-the-air television or a retransmission of a non-subscription broadcast program. Interactive and subscription services such as satellite radio, digital cable (except retransmission of broadcast television), and on-demand online music are all subject to the provision.

The amendment also provided for a collecting society for sound recording performance royalties, so that individual licensing would not be necessary. SoundExchange is a not-for-profit collective licensing organization designated by the Librarian of Congress to have exclusive authority to collect the royalties due for non-interactive digital transmissions of sound recordings. If you are a sound recording copyright holder, and your music is performed via DMCA compliant Internet radio, you are entitled to receive royalty payments from SoundExchange; see the appendix for registration and contact information for SoundExchange. On-demand online streaming is also subject to the performance right, but licenses are negotiated with each copyright holder and royalties do not flow through SoundExchange.

Part of the impetus for the DPRSRA was a fear by record labels of substitution—that consumers could get the recordings or music in a different fashion and would no longer be buying recorded music (much like their concerns in the 1920s). However, the interactive services, unlike radio, were deemed substitutive for the purchase of recordings, given their on-demand nature. As Robert Gorman and Jane Ginsburg note in their treatise on copyright:

> *What precipitated the amendment was the introduction of technology allowing for digital audio transmissions to home subscribers (fully akin to cable-television subscribers) who receive the sounds of top quality digital sound recordings and who may well thus forego the purchase of cassettes and compact discs. In part it was assumed that many digital-audio subscribers would indulge in home taping. It was understood by the congressional proponents of the legislation that "interactive" audio services would allow subscribers to call up any desired digital recordings at any time (i.e., pay-per-listen or audio-on-demand, the equivalent of pay-per-view for cable subscribers) and thus altogether displace the need to purchase recordings.*[1]

ROYALTIES ON WEBCASTS

The DPRSRA created an uproar in 2007 when the Copyright Royalty Board substantially increased fees for DMCA-compliant Internet radio. Independent broadcasters, as well as larger online stations from public radio, are obligated under the new compensation scheme to pay a flat per song per play rate plus a per "station" fee. As a result of the outcry that such a system would effectively shutter most online radio stations, legislators introduced the Internet Radio Equality Act, which would have lowered fees back to a more manageable rate. In the interim, SoundExchange, which collects and distributes the royalties, agreed to terms with smaller webcasters that would require them to pay 10 or 12 percent of revenues or 7 percent of expenses, whichever is higher, and also established a cap of $50,000 in annual fees that would be due from any single webcaster, including large services like Yahoo!

1　Gorman, Robert and Ginsburg, Jane C. *Copyright: Cases and Materials.* Fifth Edition. Charlottesville: Lexis Law Publishing, 1999

Another distinction between musical works and sound recordings lies in section 114 of the Copyright Act, which sets forth limitations on rights in sound recordings. One provision makes it explicitly clear that an owner of a sound recording has no authority to prevent others from creating a sound recording with similar sounds. This means that no record label can prevent another from recording a cover of a song, as long as the owner of the copyright in the musical work properly authorizes such a recording.

> The exclusive rights of the owner of copyright in a sound recording under clauses (1) and (2) of section 106 do not extend to the making or duplication of another sound recording that consists entirely of an independent fixation of other sounds, even though such sounds imitate or simulate those in the copyrighted sound recording.

—Copyright Act of 1976, 17 U.S.C § 114(b)

USE OF MUSIC IN TELEVISION, VIDEO GAMES, AND FILM

As the music industry has changed, so have outlets for the release and delivery of music to listeners. One shift has been the recent dramatic increase in the amount of music used in television, film, and videogames.

Despite the differences in the two types of music copyrights, the use of music in film and television is rather simple. Both the copyright for sound recordings and musical works are entitled to payment streams, with a few differences.

Two rights are needed to include the musical compositions in an audiovisual work: (a) the right to synchronize the music with the video (commonly called the "synch license"), and (b) a license to publicly perform the music. The synchronization license is granted by the publisher or copyright owner, and gives the licensee the right to attach the music to the video (or synchronize it). It's usually a flat fee paid to the copyright owner.

The broadcast or public performance of the audiovisual work containing the musical composition will trigger royalty payments to the applicable PRO, resulting in the second stream of revenue. Note that no royalties are collected for public performance of the musical composition when the audiovisual work is shown in theaters, however.

Sound recordings are licensed via a master use license, which grants the video owner the right to use the master recording in the audiovisual work. Public performance royalties may also be applicable if the broadcast is a digital transmission, under the DPRSRA. Finally, don't forget that DVDs, videogames, and sales of videos through digital downloads all require a mechanical license for the reproduction of the musical composition.

SHOULD I LET MY RECORD LABEL DO MY SYNCHRONIZATION LICENSE DEALS?

A record label that has been courting our band since our tour last summer finally sent me a letter agreement pursuant to which they want me to agree to give them all synchronization license rights for a 25 percent share that would come to me. Should I sign it?

Answer: *It depends. As with all record label deal negotiations, what you decide to do here depends on what party has the leverage in the negotiations. If you are well positioned, this is something that you should push back on. Record labels rarely, if ever, play a role in finding or negotiating what can be profitable synchronization deals; this is something typically done by a music publisher appointed to the task by the original author (or artist) or by the artist themselves. It is, in our general opinion, unreasonable for a record label to take any of these royalties, and certainly not 75 percent. We recommend that you push back on this term and try to keep this royalty pool to yourself. At minimum, you should keep the majority and let the label have 25 percent provided that they play some role in finding and/or negotiating for this license.*

In practice, using Guitar Hero as an example, Harmonix (the manufacturer of the popular Guitar Hero and Rock Band videogames) must procure mechanical licenses and pay royalties to the owner of the musical composition copyright for the sales of each game that contains the composition. They'll also need a synchronization license to synchronize the composition to the visual images in the game, and a master use license for any portions of the sound recording they may use. This is all in addition to the rights to use the artist's name, and in some cases, their image.

SAMPLING

Sampling another's music on your own record also requires licenses for the use of the master recording and musical composition. The musical composition copyright holder and the sound recording copyright owner will require a payment of royalties, but this amount is often based on the extent of the use in the new material. Licenses for samples are typically negotiated on a case-by-case basis and in the case of musical compositions usually results in the owner of the sampled composition being given a negotiated percentage of the newly created work.

IS A SAMPLE INFRINGING?

Somebody told me that if our band uses less than five seconds of another song as a sample, we don't need to get that cleared. Is that true? What can happen if we don't get it cleared?

Answer: *No, this is not true. There is no minimum duration that triggers a need for a license. As has been shown in litigation, even a couple of notes can be considered a sample that requires a license to be legally used.*

MASH-UPS AND EDITABLE TRACKS

Some artists are now offering multitrack downloads of songs, which allow fans to create their own remixes of the material. (Trent Reznor made news when his band Nine Inch Nails released a number of multitrack files to his fans for free.) Other downloadable and online programs allow users to mix two songs together, creating a combination of the two (or more) songs together. With the sound recording copyright owner's permission, this is perfectly legal.

However, when songs and individual instrument tracks are remixed without copyright permission, a question of legality arises. The new material is clearly a derivative work of the original song(s), but is it a fair use? What is the impact of the new song on the market for original material? As of the time of press, the analysis of a fair use defense for mash-ups has yet to be decided by a court of law. Stay tuned, as this is sure to be an interesting topic in years to come.

CHAPTER 4

What Is a "Copy" and What Is a "Performance?"

As mentioned earlier, two of the exclusive rights provided to a copyright holder are the rights to:

1. copy or control the copying of his or her work and
2. control the distribution of copies of a work.

In a world of digital distribution and computer files, how do you define a "copy" when the copy is in soft copy, rather than hard copy? This question is one of the largest challenges posed today by digital distribution. For example, the first sale doctrine would seem to indicate that a person can sell his or her "copy" of a sound recording, but how would this apply online? It's theoretically

---

CAN YOU SELL iTUNES FILES?

Joe Smith buys a copy of the Dixie Chicks' "I Can Love You Better" from the iTunes music store. Joe later decides he wants to sell his soft copy of the song to Janet Williams. Can he do this?

Answer: *Theoretically, under the first sale doctrine, Joe can sell his copy, but he'll have to delete his copy. However, it would be impossible for Joe to actually give his file to Janet without also giving her his device on which the song was loaded, because a copy would be necessary. Even if Joe deletes the song from his computer as soon as he's sent the file to Janet, he has still infringed the right of the copyright holder to restrict copying of the work. Any sale of the iTunes file would also be subject to the terms of service that Joe Smith agreed to when buying the song from Apple.*

impossible, today, to transfer a file to another without making a new copy of it before deleting the original. Therefore, the first sale doctrine becomes impossible to apply to soft copies transmitted to another person, because it's not the original file.

Copying is also an issue for companies who provide digital delivery services. The concept of a "server copy," or copies created internally by music services to facilitate their delivery of music (oftentimes copies will be needed on multiple computer servers) has been the subject of much discussion as technology develops. As of early 2009, there is still a dispute regarding the requirement of mechanical licenses for "server copies" for online music services.

The Copyright Act does, however, stipulate that it is not infringement for broadcast services to create limited copies of copyrighted works as necessary for the purpose of facilitating their services, if the other required licenses are in place:

- *Notwithstanding the provisions of section 106, and except in the case of a motion picture or other audiovisual work, it is not an infringement of copyright for a transmitting organization entitled to transmit to the public a performance or display of a work, under a license, including a statutory license under section 114(f), or transfer of the copyright or under the limitations on exclusive rights in sound recordings specified by section 114(a) or for a transmitting organization that is a broadcast radio or television station licensed as such by the Federal Communications Commission and that makes a broadcast transmission of a performance of a sound recording in a digital format on a non-subscription basis, to make no more than one copy or phonorecord of a particular transmission program embodying the performance or display, if: the copy or phonorecord is retained and used solely by the transmitting organization that made it, and no further copies or phonorecords are reproduced from it; and*
- *the copy or phonorecord is used solely for the transmitting organization's own transmissions within its local service area, or for purposes of archival preservation or security; and*

- *unless preserved exclusively for archival purposes, the copy or phonorecord is destroyed within six months from the date the transmission program was first transmitted to the public.*
                                                        —*Copyright Act of 1976, 17 U.S.C § 112(a)*

Further, in section 112(e) of the Copyright Act, Congress provided for a statutory right of the broadcaster to make the copy allowed in section 112(a), so that the broadcaster need not seek permission and a license each time they need a "server copy."[1] The right is conditioned upon the organization retaining and using it, and destroying the server copy within six months of the sound recording's first transmission to the public.

Despite Congress's provision for the broadcasting industry, we believe that the concept of a "server copy" is still an unresolved issue for digital and online services.

WHY IS IT OKAY TO COPY MY MUSIC FROM CD ONTO MY COMPUTER, BUT I CAN'T SHARE IT?

Copyright protects covered works from unauthorized copying. When you place a compact disc into your computer and create a file of the music on that CD, you are technicially creating a copy of the music file onto the hard drive of your computer, and that a copy is unauthorized unless specifically noted otherwise in the accompanying CD materials. So why don't music companies seem to care about this type of copying, when making copy of the file for sharing is so targeted?

The answer is somewhat murky. Technically, it may be a violation of copyright law, but as long as you don't share the copy and you are creating a copy for personal use only, the RIAA seems to look the other way. Their Web site says such copying "won't usually raise concerns"[2] if it's for personal use only, meaning that record labels seem less concerned about copying a CD into a different format than copies created and distributed. While some labels have experimented with copy protection built into CDs to prevent this very type of copying, such protection is not in widespread use. Again, as evidenced by their lawsuits against individuals for Internet piracy, the RIAA's level of interest raises significantly if you start sharing those files.

---

1   *Copyright Act of 1976, 17 U.S.C § 112(e)*
2   http://www.riaa.com/physicalpiracy.php?content_selector=piracy_online_the_law

WHAT IS A "PERFORMANCE?"

In addition to a "copy," we have discussed the concept of a "public performance" as it applies to both musical works and sound recordings. Copyright law officially defines a public performance or display:

> To perform or display a work publicly means:
>
> - To perform or display it at a place open to the public or at any place where a substantial number of persons outside of a normal circle of a family and its social acquaintances is gathered; or
> - To transmit or otherwise communicate a performance or display of the work to a place specified by clause (1) or to the public, by means of any device or process, whether the members of the public capable of receiving the performance or display receive it in the same place or in separate places and at the same time or at different times.

—*Copyright Act of 1976, 17 U.S.C. §101*

Therefore, performance royalties can be derived by both live performances of musical compositions, as well as certain transmissions. This right is limited, however, depending on the type of copyright. Remember, sound recording copyright holders have only those rights under sections 106 (1), (2), (3), and (6), and there exists no right of public performance under section 106 (4) for sound recordings.

Streams and Downloads

As the distribution of music has moved online, questions have been raised about whether a stream is a performance or a download, or both, given that a data file must be downloaded into a computer's cache in order to play the stream on the computer. The Copyright Office considers a stream to qualify for performance and mechanical royalties, as confirmed by the recent ruling by the Copyright Royalty Board (and apparent approval by the Copyright Office) that set royalty rates for streaming and tethered downloads.

ASCAP and BMI have also argued that a permanent digital download also has a public performance royalty attached (and have lost in court so far). If read literally, however, the definition of "performance" includes the "transmission" of the work, and any download must technically be "transmitted" to the buyer. All these lingering questions continue to highlight the ambiguity over how copyright should be applied online. We'll address these questions, and how artists and writers get paid from digital performances starting in chapter 7.

CHAPTER 5

Copyright Law and Ever-Changing Distribution Models

While Congress has tried to anticipate future delivery schemes for music and other copyrighted works, wholesale changes to copyright law cannot occur on a dime. Distribution models and payment schemes change nearly every year to accompany transforming technologies and a continuous stream of new offerings. And as we have seen so far, a number of various stakeholders are affected, and each must appropriately implement measures to ensure compliance with any new copyright legislation.

One recent example of technology exposing deficiencies in old definitions and their subsequent impacts can be seen with the case of the ringtone. As we discussed, copyright law provides for the statutory mechanical license rate (currently 9.1 cents per song) to be paid to the writer/publisher of a song. Prior to a Copyright Office ruling in the fall of 2006, publishers were typically receiving up to 10 percent of the retail price for the sale of a ringtone containing their musical composition through their negotiations with wireless providers, which on a $2.99 ringtone could equate to nearly 30 cents per ringtone sold. However, in their ruling, the Copyright Office declared that ringtones are subject to the compulsory mechanical license—and that rate is 9.1 cents, significantly less than the 30 cents to which publishers had became accustomed. Susan Butler summarized the issue in *Billboard:*

> *Publishers could lose substantial revenue as a result of the October 16 decision. Currently, negotiated market rates to license compositions for ringtones is the greater of 10 cents or 10 percent of the retail price. With ringtones retailing around $2, publishers*

receive about 20 cents. But the statutory rate is 9.1 cents for a compulsory license to reproduce compositions for digital phonorecord deliveries (DPD)—which includes ringtones, the Copyright Office now says. "As long as the ringtone is merely an excerpt of a musical work or of a pre-existing sound recording, then the composition used for the ringtone is subject to the compulsory license," Register of Copyrights Marybeth Peters wrote in the 35-page decision. [1]

Fortunately for music publishers, when the Copyright Royalty Board set rates for streaming in late 2008, it also assigned a 24-cent mechanical rate to ringtones.

COPYRIGHT LAW AND THE RINGTONE

The growing popularity of ringtones has highlighted gaps in copyright definitions. Copyright law provides for a statutory mechanical license rate of 9.1 cents per copy of a composition embodied in a track delivered or sold. (This rate is adjusted for inflation from time to time, usually every two to three years.) However, this is not a good fit with the ringtone market, as ringtones are typically sold at a premium and do not embody an entire composition. Naturally, with the raging popularity of these products (which became a multi-billion dollar industry in less than a decade), the numerous stakeholders have been tireless in their efforts to arrive at an appropriate rate.

Up until quite recently, publishers were typically receiving up to 10 percent of the retail price for the sale of a ringtone, which could vary wildly depending on the sale price. In 2006, the Copyright Office ruled that ringtones were subject to the compulsory mechanical license, which for digital phonorecords is the established flat rate of 9.1 cents. Naturally, publishers were not pleased with this outcome.

In 2008, the Copyright Royalty Board established statutory rates for the reproduction of musical compositions as part of the sale or distribution of ringtones at 24 cents. Needless to say, this was quite a victory for music publishers. This rate will endure for the period between January 1, 2008 through December 31, 2012.

---

1   Butler, Susan. "Ringtone Rates Set." *Billboard.* 28 October 2006.

Another deficiency often decried by online music providers is the lack of a comprehensive clearinghouse for mechanical licenses for services who stream music online. Currently, HFA clears mechanical licenses for approximately 37,000 individual publishers, but this does not provide close to the 100 percent clearance sought by most major digital music services. Until recently, this left music services in the unpleasant and costly position of having to negotiate separately with each of the remaining publishers for each musical composition offered on their service. At time of press, there are several mechanical clearing services emerging in the marketplace, a couple of which show promise of filling the desperate need of several U.S. digital music services. It is a long standing hope in the industry that at one point the entire process of clearing mechanical royalties for online services (including subscription services) will be streamlined via proper handling through a central "one stop" entity of some kind. On a related note, so-called "section 115 reform" has been at the forefront of concerns for a number of companies, since the process of finding and negotiating so many licenses is often unwieldy and cost-prohibitive. For details on the outcome of the process, refer to page 93.

Finally, the lawsuit by ASCAP seeking a performance right in a download further illustrates the difficulties posed by antiquated laws that are often interpreted to the benefit of each reader. Rights holders continue to seek more revenue as a result of the ambiguity of the law applied to emerging distribution methods, leading primarily to a windfall for lawyers, rather than copyright owners. One of the prevailing practices for new online businesses has been to start a service that may or may not be legal under current law, attract a significant user base, get sued, and use the user base as leverage in negotiations to obtain legitimate license from rights owners.

Further complicating matters are the logistical hurdles that stand in the way of copyright reform. Often, legislation is held up in committee or not passed due to the efforts of lobbyists with opposing interests. For example, the radio broadcasters lobbying group is considered to be among the largest and most powerful in Washington, and they have defeated every attempt to date to assign a performance right to sound recordings, which could result in significant new revenue for labels and artists.

IS THE CRB UNCONSTITUTIONAL?

As we go to press in the fall of 2009, a challenge to the constitutionality of the Copyright Royalty Board (CRB)—the second in two years—threatens to throw into disarray what little stability the industry has achieved via the CRB. Specifically, the plaintiffs allege that the CRB is unconstitutional due to its running afoul of the Appointments Clause of the United States constitution. If successful, the suit could possibly invalidate all CRB rate decisions to date. Among those relying on CRB-established rates, most are hoping that even if this scenario were to come to fruition, there would be a Congressional act of some kind to legitimize the rates and maintain the current status quo. Worst case scenario, it is possible that artists, writers, licensors, and distributors would be left with substantial ambiguity about their revenues and expenses on a retroactive and going forward basis.

Despite the best efforts of legislators, it is impossible to anticipate every technology change and new business model for distribution. As we move forward in the digital age, lawmakers will need to be ever vigilant about the law, and music industry professionals will need to be ever creative to find new methods of licensing.

PART II

Music Law in the Digital Age

CHAPTER 6

Digital Distribution Channels and Mediums

As detailed in chapter 1, the distribution medium of choice for music has evolved dramatically since music was first recordable in the late 1800s. By far, the most phenomenal shift in distribution of music came with the wide adoption of the Internet in the past fifteen years. First taking off in the late 1990s, in association with illegal sites such as the original Napster, online distribution of music has flourished.

There are currently well over five hundred legitimate digital music services worldwide offering over 10 million tracks—over five times the stock of a music megastore. Despite this growth, online piracy has consistently dwarfed online sales by a ratio of 20:1.[1] The numbers continue to shift, however, and online legal sales and other forms of distribution continue to gain traction. As of 2009, at least a few record labels are informally confirming that digital sales are finally exceeding physical sales.

While the actual numbers may vary, one thing is for sure: the digital music industry is growing. Even the term "digital music industry" is a bit of a misnomer, since it is really just a facet of the greater music industry. The "digital" term merely refers to the fact that consumers are getting the music online. The term "Internet company" eventually faded, as the market realized that "Internet" was merely the medium, and we suspect that "digital music industry" too will fade in popularity as online consumption continues to grow and become more common.

In 2008, digital sales in the United States and Canada exceeded one billion tracks (note that the term "track" commonly refers to

---

1 IFPI, Digital Music Report 2008, Jan 2008, http://ifpi.org

single sound recordings of a single song as sold on the Internet). This is a 27 percent increase in sales over 2007. According to Sound-Scan, online album sales also spiked 32 percent over the prior year with 65.8 million full albums sold online in the same territories.

It does appear that online sales are growing at a rate faster than physical sales are dropping.[2] By way of illustration, for the 2006 to 2007 year, CD sales dropped 20.5 percent while digital track sales went up 43.2 percent. Despite the optimism from higher percentage gains in track sales, the overall numbers bear a different story, because digital track sales on a dollar basis still fall dramatically short of CD sales in the past few years. The recording industry consistently uses these numbers to show their dramatic year over year losses. However, it is important to remember that they are using the 1990s as a benchmark—a period when (1) sales were inflated due to many consumers' attempts to replace their existing music collection with CDs, and (2) the cost of CDs was at its highest in the 1990s at approximately $17 each for mainstream content (in the context of a booming economy).[3]

Regardless of where one falls in the industry—a record label executive, an artist, a start-up in the entertainment space, a songwriter—this increase in digital sales and distribution will continue to shape the industry and market as we know them. So, how does one succeed—or even survive—in this quickly evolving field of creation, practice, or business?

Getting to the bottom of some fundamental questions is a good start for any rights holder, creator, businessperson, or visionary seeking to survive and thrive in the current market. How is music distributed online? How do artists, labels, music publishers, and digital distributors get paid? How can one control distribution of their works on the Internet? Is it still possible to make a living in the music business despite the incredible losses due to online piracy?

Although imperfect in its application and certainly wrought with flaws, copyright law and the businesses that depend on its enforcement have generally adapted to accommodate innovations in the music business.

---

2 RIAA, 2007 Manufacturers' Unit Shipments and Value Chart, http://www.riaa.com/keystatistics.php

3 RIAA, 2007 Manufacturers' Unit Shipments and Value Chart, http://www.riaa.com/keystatistics.php

We will now shift into diving deeper into music law in the digital context of our era. Specifically, we will summarize the current distribution channels and mediums and how they interact with U.S. copyright law. We'll also explore current and future business models for music distribution via online and mobile channels including a look at the "Web 2.0" phenomenon. With this analysis, we'll also assist in identifying where copyright law has failed us in providing a suitable framework for rights allocation and associated royalties. Last but not least, we'll apply some of these considerations to the international context: how do these rights translate across borders? All in all, you will be equipped with a vocabulary and deeper understanding of how the current system works, and is likely to work, in years to come.

DIGITAL DISTRIBUTION OF MUSIC

There is little question that music's grand entrance to the online distribution and the Internet era generally was an unlawful one. The ushering parties, Napster and other peer-to-peer or "P2P" sites, made it extremely easy and cheap (free) for online users to acquire and consume music often without a trace, and in almost all cases, without compensating the copyright owners for the protected uses of their works.

In response to the overwhelming growth of piracy, the RIAA has sued individual file sharers, and copyright holders have sued the companies providing the mechanisms that enable file sharing online. At least two of the notable court cases that came as a result have helped to shape our understanding of legal distribution of music online. Specifically, the Napster and Grokster cases (decided in 2001 and 2005, respectively) helped to define what is and is not permitted online. You can read more about these cases in chapter 8.

While these two cases were making their way through the judicial system, a number of legal music services were developing their own legal services. Among them was Apple.

When Apple launched its online digital download store iTunes in 2003, it was one of thirty legitimate digital music services that were operating worldwide by the end of that year.[4] By the end of 2004,

---

4 *Digital Music Report*, IFPI, 2008

there were over fifty established online music sites in Europe and over one hundred worldwide.[5] Despite the obvious challenges that accompany competing with free, Apple was confident in the role it would play in the music industry. Armed with content license deals with the (then) five major record labels amounting to a 200,000+ track-strong library, Apple had a public goal of selling one million tracks within one month. It was a surprise to all, including Apple, when they reached this goal in a mere week. Six years later, Apple is the uncontested industry leader in track sales (and the third largest music retailer in the U.S. overall), having sold over five billion songs—the vast majority of global online track sales. Despite their market dominance, their store is one of hundreds of legitimate online stores worldwide.

In addition to a growing number of retail channels, Internet distribution and mobile technology have made additional formats available for artist releases. Beyond the well known physical formats (CDs, records, etc.), artist releases can now be packaged and sold in multiple formats available online, including video downloads, conditional downloads, on-demand streams, music videos, DRM-free MP3s, ringtones, or mobile full-track downloads. For example, sales of Justin Timberlake's *Future Sex/Love Sounds* album, released in September 2006, comprised 115 products that sold a total of 19 million units, of which only 20 percent were in CD format. To put this into perspective, in 2003, there were less than ten formats available per artist release, dominated by the CD and cassette. By 2008, there were over 100 formats available.[6]

While online P2P networks remain the primary source of digital music distribution online, legal digital music stores and services continue to gain traction, year after year.

Let's examine the current offerings and business models available.

WHO IS MAKING MONEY IN THE "DIGITAL MUSIC INDUSTRY?"

Who is making money in the "digital music industry?" For a long time, the mainstream answer was quite simple: Apple. But while Apple prevails as the best-known success story, its primary revenues do not

---

5   "Summary Update on Legitimate Services," 2003, www.ifpi.org
6   *Digital Music Report*, IFPI, 2008

stem from music sales or music distribution. Apple's fiscal and brand success is a direct result of its phenomenal hardware sales, specifically the iPod and the iPhone. It is evident that the iTunes store is a mere loss leader in the business with absolutely tiny margins in comparison to what the company earns in hardware sales.

Until 2008, there was little dispute that the music industry was ailing in this digital or "Internet" age. It was hard to find a professional conference or other event addressing the subject of digital music sales at which at least one speaker did not lament the "unjust" gains Apple has enjoyed due to iPod sales. There was somewhat of a collective frustration among everyone from artists to industry executives that the only company making money in the music business was the company making the hardware consumers used to store and play previously purchased or stolen music.

WHAT'S ON AN iPOD?

Are iPods only used to hold purchased iTunes tracks? Sources vary, but at least one claims that the average iPod has 1,770 tracks stored on it, and with very conservative estimates, an average of 800 were copied without an appropriate sale or license.[7] With many millions of iPods in the marketplace, that is a lot of stolen music—and these are conservative estimates.

Doom and gloom aside, the focus seems to have finally shifted. The area of interest and opportunity in the industry now lies in emerging business models for the distribution and consumption of music and a range of music-related products. After years of fighting online piracy and restricting new business models offered by companies such as eMusic, RealNetworks, Yahoo, YouTube, and others, music rights holders (record labels and music publishers) seem to be finally coming around and supporting the innovation needed to sustain their revenues. A number of new initiatives are showing increased creativity and a desire to make the rules of the game, rather than playing someone else's.

---

7 Guy Dixon, "Average iPod has 800 Illegal Tracks," VNUENET.com, 2008

NO MORE SUING GRANDMOTHERS AND YOUNG KIDS?

The RIAA expended significant resources suing individual infringers in recent years—as many as 35,000 lawsuits since 2003. The approach has been largely ineffective and resulted in a terrible public relations mess. The trade organization seems to have filed the last suit of its kind in August of 2008 and is instead now seeking to partner with Internet service providers pursuant to which it will be able to warn infringers without having to win the battle for such names' identities.

> The new approach dispenses with one of the most contentious parts of the lawsuit strategy, which involved filing lawsuits requiring ISPs to disclose the identities of file sharers. Under the new strategy, the RIAA would forward its e-mails to the ISPs without demanding to know the customers' identities.[8]

Whether this new approach will be effective remains to be seen. At least, we will be spared the collective whine regarding the outcomes of the previous litigation strategy.

---

8 McBride, Sarah and Ethan Smith, "Music Industry to Abandon Mass Suits," *Wall Street Journal*, December 19, 2008, at B1.

CHAPTER 7

Digital Music Delivery Formats

	Permanent Downloads	Conditional Downloads	On-Demand Streaming	Internet Radio
Sound Recording Rights	Wholesale rates are negotiated with each label/licensor; typically per track/album	Variable rates are negotiated with each label/licensor; typically per play or revenue share	Variable rates are negotiated with each label/licensor; typically per play or revenue share	Compulsory rates typically paid to Sound-Exchange (generally on a per performance or hourly basis)
Reproduction Right/ Mechanical	Compulsory Rate: 9.1 cents per track or 1.75 cents/minute (through 2012)	Generally, 10.5% of service revenue	Generally, 10.5% of service revenue (minus PRO fees)	Current Dispute: is there a mechanical for server copies?
Public Performance Right for Musical Compositions	None, as there is no public performance attributed to downloads	None, per recent decisions, as there is no public performance attributable to a conditional download	Yes, negotiated with each PRO	Yes, negotiated with each PRO

Fig. 7.1. Licensing Models for Various Digital Music Offerings

As we have seen, the music business derives income from a variety of rights that entitle copyright holders to a plethora of assorted revenue streams. Going online, depending on the delivery format, different copyrights apply with different rates, and different rights holders or administrators are paid accordingly. This chapter will describe the four mainstream digital music delivery formats and explain the copyright licensing implications for each. (Note that illegal P2P offerings are not addressed here. Services such as LimeWire and the Pirate Bay operate by facilitating a connection between two individual users who wish to "share" their files. This section concerns legitimate, legal distribution of music done with the consent of the associated rights holders.)

PERMANENT DOWNLOADS

Permanent downloads are also known as "tracks," "MP3s," and "downloads."

Functionality

Permanent downloads are tracks or songs that are delivered via the Internet and can be stored and played from digital music or "MP3" players, mobile phones, a computer's hard drive, or a compact disc. Permanent downloads are generally purchased from online stores in a format superior to what one typically finds on a P2P site, typically with a higher bit rate and no imperfections. Companies that sell permanent downloads include iTunes, eMusic, RealNetworks/ Rhapsody, Napster, and Amazon. Formats vary.

Most stores selling tracks between 2002 and 2008 were selling files with DRM. Often required by record labels, DRM functions to limit the end users' ability to copy the file, among other things. In 2008, several popular online stores, including iTunes, Amazon, and RealNetworks/Rhapsody, prevailed in obtaining licenses from record labels that allowed them to distribute permanent downloads "DRM-free," as MP3s. This long-awaited shift allows users to play downloads on a broader range of hardware—most importantly, iPods. Until late 2008, Apple had refused to sell tracks without its proprietary DRM or license its technology to others, which limited the interoperability of various stores' content and hardware devices.

Business Model

The business model for permanent downloads is simple, generally. Online distributors pay a wholesale rate for tracks/albums and control retail pricing themselves, keeping the margin as a small profit. Some stores, however, offer a certain number of permanent downloads per month for a bulk fee. (As of 2009, eMusic was the most prevalent example of this.)

From the launch of its iTunes store in 2003 until early 2009, Apple maintained the standard fee for online track sales with the vast majority of online tracks selling for $0.99 each. The iTunes store is now selling tracks and albums with varied pricing schemes for track downloads at the behest of labels.

COST PER TRACK

Perhaps as a result of distributor-side marketing research, or perhaps as a result of pressure from record labels, in late 2008 and early 2009 the major download retail stores started to adjust their retail prices for track sales. Instead of all tracks selling for $0.99, the stores are now selling tracks for a range of prices, generally ranging from $0.69 to $1.29 each. We believe it is reasonable to expect that the market will continue to further evolve so as to set prices based on the demand for the content.

Licensing

Obtaining licenses for digital download distribution is generally a simple one-stop affair. Distribution companies enter into agreements with record labels for the right to distribute the sound recording and then pay the record labels a license or "wholesale" fee to cover both the sound recording and the composition (mechanical) license.

THE WORD "LICENSE"

Natalie works in the label relations department of a large company with a digital music service division. She has noticed that in some of the company's content license agreements with record labels, the labels insist on deleting the word "license" from throughout the agreement and replacing it with "distribution" or "permission" or some other similar term. Why do they do this? It is usually the more sophisticated labels that make this change.

Answer: *Record labels do not like to refer to agreements intended to govern distributors' sale as "license" agreements (even though there is a license being granted to make and sell copies of the sound recordings), as different contractual terms apply to distribution of music in agreements between record labels and artists depending on whether the distribution is a "sale" or a "license." Historically, record labels shared any revenue from the licensing of music 50/50. This was the case as there was an assumption that the artist played an active/lead role in seeking out licensing opportunities while record labels were primarily focused on marketing, tours, and record sales. On the other hand, the agreements between record labels and artists allowed for relatively small royalties for album sales—typically an 11 or 12 percent royalty rate, but an established artist can command a royalty as high as 17 to 18 percent. As a result, if record labels enter into agreements with digital music services that license such services to distribute downloads, an artist with a traditional contract could successfully claim that they are entitled to 50 percent of attributable revenue—significantly more than the few cents they typically collect for download sales today.*

In fact, major record labels have been sued on this point. However, in a case decided in March of 2009 involving Eminem and Universal Music Group, a federal jury in Los Angeles sided with major labels when they denied to pay royalties on downloads of Eminem recordings at the "50 percent master license royalty" rate.

The producers of some early Eminem recordings and the producers' manager both had an interest in royalty payments on some of Eminem's early recordings, and had sued UMG. At trial, UMG used Amazon as an example, and drew a correlation between the company as a retailer of both CDs and digital downloads to convince the jurors that the sale of both products provided the same end result for the consumer—ownership of a copy of an Eminem recording. The jury ultimately found that permanent downloads are "records sold through normal retail channels," and thus royalties should be paid to Eminem and the producers based on the much lower rate.

ARE DOWNLOADS PERFORMANCES?

ASCAP has attempted in court to have a public performance royalty attributed to a permanent download, due to the statutory construction of copyright law and the definition of "public performance" including "transmissions." To date, ASCAP has been unsuccessful with its efforts. In a court decision in 2007 that ASCAP lost, the court noted:

> *Surely ASCAP would not contend that if a retail purchaser of musical records begins audibly playing each tape or disc as soon as he receives it the vendor is engaging in a public performance. Neither does a performance occur in the situation at issue herein, for it is not the availability of prompt replay but the simultaneously perceptible nature of a transmission that renders it a performance under the Act.*
>
> *The statutory language itself, however, makes clear that the transmission of a performance, rather than just the transmission of data constituting a media file, is required in order to implicate the public performance right in a copyrighted work.*
>
> *—U.S. v. ASCAP 485 F. Supp. 2d 438 (S.D.N.Y. 2007)*

The decision is subject to appeal in the Second Circuit at the time of press.

While selling permanent downloads is definitely the simplest way to distribute music online, simplicity does not necessarily mean profit. Margins on download sales are typically quite small, and companies in this business have one very tough competitor that only continues to grow in size: P2P offerings. As demonstrated by Apple with the iPod/iTunes model, download sales are best supported if offered in conjunction with an attractive hardware offering or as an add-on to other digital music offerings such as subscription or radio services.

CONDITIONAL DOWNLOADS

Conditional downloads are also known as "tethered downloads," "limited downloads," or "to go subscription/streaming."

Functionality

Conditional downloads are essentially time-limited downloads or "portable" streams. In 2004, Microsoft released "Janus," a digital-rights management technology that allowed for subscription content to be playable at the associated reduced rates on a personal handheld player or a computer without having to be connected to the Internet. Basically, subscribers to services that offer these types of tracks have the ability to export subscription content onto their players. Provided that the subscriber's account stays current and they are able to "synch" the device at least once every thirty days, the content functions as a permanently downloaded content. Content is playable for thirty days after each synch, so failure to synch or maintain a subscription will result in disabling of the content on the player or hard drive.

Business Model

Conditional downloads are typically made available via a subscription offering. Users pay anywhere from $10 to $15 per month for "unlimited" access to a company's catalog. Companies that have offered this service include Napster, Microsoft, Rhapsody (RealNetworks), and Yahoo Music.

The business model varies, depending on the specifics of the agreements between the record label and the digital music distributor. In general, record labels and music publishers are paid royalties based on usage, revenues, or subscribers, with a broad range of terms attributable to each. Depending on the royalty scheme, a licensor may benefit from high usage, high revenue (subscription and advertising), or a high volume of subscribers. Artists and other rights holders are paid pursuant to the terms of the appropriate governing agreement.

Licensing

The licensing scheme for conditional downloads can get quite complicated. Unlike the "one-stop shop" approach available for distribution of digital downloads, a digital distributor handling clearances for distribution of conditional downloads must typically obtain two licenses: one from the record label for the distribution of the sound recording and one from the music publisher for the limited reproduction of the composition. (This is true at the time of press. At least one significant PRO is pursuing performance royalties in connection with these offerings.)

SECTION 115 ISSUES

Until late 2008, several subscription and ad supported digital-music services were operating with unknown costs, as there was no agreed-upon rate for mechanicals due, if any, for conditional downloads and on-demand streams. It was a point of great frustration in the industry for many years. Can you imagine any other business where goods are sold with an unknown cost? It was akin to selling Internet or cell phone services for a monthly fee, not knowing what the seller would actually have to pay for access to the broadband necessary to deliver the service.

Finally, in 2008, the numerous entities with a stake in the outcome were granted some clarity on the question regarding mechanical royalties due in connection with online distribution of music. The completion of the Section 115 Copyright Royalty Board proceedings and related settlement resulted in rates that apply both retroactively and on a going-forward basis.

For standalone portable subscription services offering conditional or "tethered" downloads and on demand streaming after January 1, 2008, a distributor must pay the appropriate publisher or licensing entity the greater of three numbers for mechanical royalties:

1. 10.5 percent of revenue minus PRO payments (if any),
2. the lesser of (a) $0.80 per subscriber per month or
   (b) 21 percent of label payments, in each case minus PRO payments, or
3. $0.50 per subscriber per month.

For distributions before January 1, 2008, (1) above is 8.5 percent of revenue minus PRO payments and (2)(b) is 17 percent of label payments minus PRO payments.

However, despite the ruling on the rates, there still exists no single "one-stop" clearinghouse for mechanical licenses required to deliver content online. This is problematic for services that, without it, find themselves needing to clear licenses with hundreds—possibly even thousands—of individual publishers.

SUBSCRIPTION SERVICES V. DOWNLOADS

Michael and his lawyer friend Jared were talking about buying music through subscription services v. downloads. Jared prefers his music via a subscription service; Michael prefers his in downloads that he owns. Jared told Michael that he really doesn't "own" the downloaded content anyway, so he should be happy with an all-you-can-eat access service instead. Is Jared right? Doesn't Michael own the music in the downloads he's purchased?

Answer: *Jared is correct in that Michael doesn't actually own any music he has in downloads (unless he owns the sound recording and the underlying composition of such music). Even when he "buys" a download, he is not buying the music; he is "buying" a copy—a copy that comes with numerous restrictions. For example, he can't play that copy publicly without paying a PRO for the public performance. He can't make a dozen copies for his friends without permission from the record label and publisher (and likely paying fees associated with the duplications). He can't use the song as background music for a video he makes without getting a synchronization license from the music publisher. It is this comfort with "access" in the place of "ownership" that the subscription music services have been hoping for as users adopt a rental model in place of an ownership one.*

It remains to be seen how the "all-you-can-eat" or "to go" model will fare in this evolving industry. As technology, devices, and catalogs improve, it may end up being a strong business model and revenue stream for all stakeholders in the industry. Either way, artists and publishers should ensure that they are being properly compensated for distribution of their works via these channels. If, for example, music you wrote and/or recorded is available on a subscription site, you should be sure you're receiving mechanical and performance royalties as listed above, as well as a master use fee for the recording.

IS IT POSSIBLE TO REMOVE CONTENT FROM THE MARKET?

An old band of mine recorded our first album ten years ago. We then broke up and "re-banded" into our current group. Somehow, the original album is available on Amazon.com and iTunes and we don't want it to be publicly available (the music isn't good and it is confusing our current growing fan base). How do we get it removed from these online stores? Can we get money from sales to date? What about Internet radio? Can we get it removed from those channels as well?

Answer: *If you are the copyright owner of the sound recording or the composition, you can use the DMCA takedown provisions set forth on page 121 to have the content removed from these legitimate online stores. You may also pursue past royalties via such procedures by contacting the licensing department of the distributor (that may refer you to the original licensing entity). The Internet radio question is a little more complicated because Internet radio is governed by the compulsory license set forth in Section 114 of the Copyright Act. Consequently, you, the copyright owner, do not need to actually grant permission for the sound recording to be played or the composition performed; the right to do so is essentially required. There are certain ways to attempt to get around this, such as approaching the various Internet radio sites one by one, but it will be much harder to achieve this removal than what can be expected with a voluntary license (downloads and on demand streams). An additional and likely more attractive option is to register with SoundExchange and PRO and collect royalties from them for the use of your sound recordings.*

ON-DEMAND STREAMS

Functionality

On-demand streams function in a manner similar to conditional downloads; however, a connection to the Internet is required for transmission. Further, access ends concurrently with one's subscription; there is no day-limited "rental" or access period.

Business Model

Like conditional downloads, on-demand streams are typically made available via a subscription offering for a monthly fee, currently anywhere from $6 to $13, depending on the service. In recent years, however, on-demand streams are increasingly offered for free to the user and funded (from a royalty standpoint) by advertising. Companies that have offered this service as a subscription offering include Napster, Microsoft, Rhapsody (RealNetworks), and Yahoo Music. Companies that have offered advertising-supported on-demand streaming services include imeem, Lala, Spotify, and MySpace Music.

Fig. 7.2. Rhapsody

Like conditional download services, the business model is variable, depending on the specifics of the agreements between the record label and the digital music distributor.

Licensing

Licensing for on-demand streaming services is handled in a manner similar to the process for conditional downloads. Distributors must obtain licenses from record labels for the sound recordings and the entities handling mechanical licensing for the reproductions of the compositions (typically a combination of the Harry Fox Agency and independent "non-Fox" publishers). On demand streaming is not subject to compulsory licensing for the sound recording under the DPRSRA.

Similar to conditional downloads, the recent Copyright Royalty Board ruling set rates for mechanical royalties due in connection with on-demand streaming. For stand-alone non-portable subscription services offering interactive streaming and conditional or "tethered" downloads beginning January 1, 2008, a distributor must pay the appropriate publisher or licensing entity the greatest of three numbers:

1. 10.5 percent of revenue minus PRO payments,
2. the lesser of (a) $0.50 per subscriber per month or (b) 21 percent of label payments, in each case minus PRO payments, or
3. $0.30 per subscriber per month.

Further, stand-alone non-portable subscription (streaming only) is the greatest of:

1. 10.5 percent of revenue minus PRO payments,
2. the lesser of (a) $0.50 per subscriber per month or (b) 22 percent of label payments, in each case minus PRO payments, or
3. $0.15 per subscriber per month.

Non-subscription ad-supported is the greatest of:

1. .5 percent of revenue minus PRO payments,
2. 22 percent of label payments

For distributions before January 1, 2008, (1) is 8.5 percent of revenue minus PRO payments and (2)(b) is 17 percent of label payments minus PRO payments.

There is an expectation among many that on-demand streaming is at the heart of the future of digital music consumption. Support for this stems from a simple value analysis: users get more for their money when they have access to a high quality service offering on-demand playback of millions of songs for less than $15 per month compared to what they get for the same investment on purchased tracks. There are several barriers to this business model taking off, including consumer understanding of the products available, the requirement of "being online," limited broadband access, poor device integration, and perhaps more than any other factor, consumer attachment to "owning" their music. For companies investing in these models, these are seen as short-term obstacles that will be overcome as technology and users become more sophisticated.

INTERNET RADIO

Functionality

Internet radio functions in a manner similar to on-demand streaming without the "on-demand" part. A listener can select a station, typically based on genre, and listen to streaming music for hours and hours on end. Many services such as Pandora offer the ability to create a station based on the listener's taste in music or selection of artists. What is different, however, is the amount of control a listener has over the content. Internet radio stations, in order to qualify for the statutory DMCA rate—a rate that is significantly cheaper than the rates for on-demand streaming or plays of conditional downloads—must adhere to such delivery requirements. Under the Digital Millennium Copyright Act, to qualify as webcaster (provider of DMCA-compliant Internet radio), a listener cannot skip more than a defined number of tracks in a period, display the identity of the tracks in the upcoming queue, play more than a defined number of tracks from a single artist/album within a defined period, and comply with other restrictions.

HOW TO SET UP AN INTERNET RADIO STATION

What do I need to do to deliver DMCA-compliant Internet radio?

Answer: *You must comply with the eligibility requirements for a statutory license to publicly perform sound recordings, as follows:*

Sound Recording Performance Complement: "DMCA-compliant radio stations" must not exceed the "sound recording performance complement." This means that in any three-hour period, the transmitting entity may play:

- no more than three songs from any particular album, or more than two such songs consecutively, and
- no more than four songs by any particular recording artist, boxed set or compilation of sound recordings (and no more than three such songs may be transmitted consecutively).

Non-Interactive: The service must be non-interactive—i.e., a user cannot receive a transmission of a program specially created for them or receive a transmission of a particular sound recording selected by them or on their behalf. (The ability of individuals to request that particular sound recordings be performed for reception by the public at large, or in the case of a subscription service, by all subscribers of the service, does not make a service interactive, if the programming on each channel of the service does not substantially consist of sound recordings that are performed within one hour of the request or at a time designated by either the transmitting entity or the individual making such request.)

Prior Announcements: The transmitting entity may not publish program schedules in advance or make prior announcements of the titles of specific songs, albums, or recording artists featured on the program. However, a transmitting entity may announce that a particular recording artist will be included within an unspecified future time period. The transmitting entity may identify the specific sound recording immediately before it is performed and may name artists as illustrative examples of the kinds of artists generally played on a particular program or station.

Textual Data: The transmission of each song must be accompanied by text identifying the title of the sound recording, the name of the phonorecord on which it can be found, and the name of the featured artist, if any.

Repeat Programming: Looped or continuous predetermined programs must be at least three hours long. Archived programs (available for Web users to hear on demand) must be at least five hours long and even then must be available to the end user for no more than two weeks. Regularly scheduled rebroadcasts of predetermined programs are permitted to occur in a two week period only three times if less than an hour in length and only four times if an hour or more in length.

Images: The service must not transmit images contemporaneously with sound recordings in a manner that suggests an affiliation or association between the sound recording copyright owner or featured artist and a particular product or service advertised by the transmitting entity.

Piracy Concerns: The transmitting entity may not cause or induce the making of a digital copy of the content, and must use technology reasonably available to it to limit the recipient from making digital copies. Further, the transmitting entity must cooperate in order to prevent any person or entity from automatically scanning the entity's transmissions in order to select a particular sound recording. Finally, the transmitting entity may not remove any DRM technology that was placed in a file by the sound recording copyright owner and must ensure such anti-theft features are not removed during the transmission process.

Already Released to Public: The transmitting entity may not transmit any sound recording that has not already been released for broadcast or sale to the public under authority of the copyright owner unless it receives permission from the copyright owner to do so.

No Channel Switching: The transmitting entity may not cause any device receiving the transmission to switch from one program channel to another.

Business Model

Like on-demand streaming, Internet radio is generally made available as a subscription or advertising-supported offering. Subscriptions run on average $5 per month while advertising-supported models are free to the end user. In general, due to the historically reasonable rates for Internet radio, the margins on Internet radio subscription products are generally better for distributors but less profitable for rights holders.

Licensing

Royalties for Internet radio are paid to SoundExchange and PROs.

In the 1990s, the DPRSRA established a "statutory" or "compulsory" license to stream sound recordings as long as the music being streamed complies with applicable restrictions. This means that services need not obtain direct licenses from each sound recording copyright owner provided that they comply with the rules and pay the appropriate royalty. Sound recording royalties are paid to Sound-Exchange, a non-profit arm of the RIAA (see chapter 3). Royalties for the performance of compositions are paid to PROs.

Despite concerns that new Section 114 radio rates are too high for Internet radio broadcasters to afford, Internet radio appears to be here to stay for a while. (See the "Royalties on Webcasts" sidebar in chapter 3.)

AD SUPPORTED

Though not a delivery format, per se, it is worth noting that any and all of the above offerings can also be made available to end users for free, legally, provided that the distributor still licenses the music and pays proper royalties to the rights holders. This can be done via an advertising-supported offering where the distributor uses the revenue from advertisements to pay the costs of license fees and running the service.

Numerous ad-supported services have been offered in the last five years; few have been particularly successful. Even YouTube and MySpace, which are technically ad-supported sites containing large amounts of music and tremendous userbases, are not overwhelmingly profitable. That said, the business model appears to continue to attract attention, with new services entering the market at least monthly. *For artists, this means that you will need to ensure that any agreements with publishing companies, record labels, or other middlemen between your work and your fans include provisions regarding royalties collected from advertising sales in addition to straight sales or subscription revenue.*

FREE/PROMOTIONAL/UPSELL OFFERINGS

Similar to the need to carefully monitor potential revenues from advertising-supported products, artists and other rights holders need to be increasingly diligent about properly licensing and collecting appropriate royalties from promotional or free offerings—offerings that are typically associated with enticing users to buy more from or subscribe to a service. For example, are you being paid when your music is being streamed in thirty-second preview clips on iTunes?

In sum, business models and distribution formats will continue to evolve. It is important for all stakeholders in the creation, licensing, and distribution chain to stay on top of this quickly evolving industry so as to ensure that they are active participants. Artists need to be on top of their agreements. Other licensors (labels, publishers) need to closely monitor their licensees, and licensees need to be proactive in the market for the business to thrive.

ROYALTIES ON MARKETING FREEBIES

I am a country artist. I write and perform my own music. My record label, the same label I have been with for fifteen years, pays me for download sales with iTunes, Amazon, and others, but I don't ever receive payments for distribution via "free" advertising-supported and subscription services, though I know my most recent albums are on at least a few of them. Where is this money going? Am I due a portion of that revenue? I know that my record label has a deal with at least two subscription services.

Answer: *It depends. If your contract with your record label specifies that you are due royalties for digital distribution of your music beyond track sales, you should be getting paid. If not, the label is rightfully keeping that revenue to itself. The best thing to do at this point is to review your contract, perhaps with the assistance of a music attorney, and determine what your best course of action is to start sharing in that revenue stream for the distribution of your works. Further, it is likely that you are due fees for the public performance of your works (if you own the compositions). You should work with the PROs with whom you are engaged in pursuit of these royalties.*

CHAPTER 8

Gaps in Copyright Law

COPYRIGHT LAW NOT MADE FOR DIGITAL AGE

Intellectual property law suffers, perhaps more than any other substantive area of law, from an inability to keep up with innovation. As technologies continue to develop and enter the marketplace at an exponential rate, current laws and guidelines struggle to keep up and protect rights holders while encouraging innovation. Copyright law is no exception.

Initially created to govern the making of physical copies of an author's works, copyright law has been particularly challenged by the Internet and the ease of copying and distribution that it allows (and in some cases, encourages). With books, music, film, software, images, videos, and numerous other forms of authored works easily duplicated and widely disseminated, often anonymously with a press of a button, it is an uphill and arguably losing battle for rights holders to try to control or monitor.

We have seen this played out in a particularly painful way in the music industry. The RIAA estimates that the music industry loses over $5 billion annually due to online piracy.[1] There are numerous potential culprits for these ongoing losses, but clearly, the current framework of charging users for individual sales or subscription access—or advertisers to display ads in places where users access content for free—is not an ideal fit for online distribution of copyrighted works.

Congress has tried to anticipate future delivery schemes for music and other copyrighted works, with legislation such as the

---

1 See details at www.riaa.org.

Digital Millennium Copyright Act, and updates to copyright law are commonly considered as a response to a specific technology, as seen earlier in the case of the DAT and the Audio Home Recording Act. Legislation was also introduced to address one of the first Web sites to serve music consumers, MP3.com, which allowed consumers to listen to copies of music that they already own from any computer connected to the Internet. Consumers merely needed to verify their ownership of a CD by inserting the CD into their computer and allowing the site to authenticate its presence. The site was eventually shut down, but it is important to any study of attempts to change the laws for the digital distribution of music online because legislation was offered specifically to make the MP3.com service legal. Amy Harmon noted in the *New York Times* that:

> *The proposed legislation is written so narrowly that it almost seems tailored to serve the specific interests of MP3.com. And no one thinks that it will pass before Congress recesses. But the bill is significant because, for the first time in this year's digital music wars, it raises the question of what is right rather than what is legal.... The company's star lawyer, David Boies, who successfully argued the Justice Department's antitrust case against Microsoft last year, has lots of arguments why Napster is blameless. What if he's right? What if existing copyright law did not envision the ability to copy on the mass scale made possible by the Internet? Does that mean that such copying should be allowed, or should the law be modified? But at a time when technology is evolving so rapidly and the stakes are so high over who can exercise how much control over copyrighted works, there may be cause for Congress to look more closely at the rights it has doled out in the past, and how those rights are being applied now.*[2]

Harmon raises a valid point. With mega-corporations controlling copyrighted works for ever-increasing copyright durations, does it make sense to continue restricting rights? On the flip side, does it spur creativity or support the health of an industry to have creative works floating around for free? These are some examples of the weighty questions that must be asked every time a change to the law is contemplated.

---

2 Harmon, Amy. "New Economy: With music widely available online, is it now time to tighten copyright laws or consider rewriting them to reflect reality?" *The New York Times.* 2 October 2000.

SIGNIFICANT LITIGATION

A&M Records et al. v. Napster, decided by the Ninth Circuit Court of Appeals in 2001, is probably the most recognizable case to be decided on copyright and digital distribution of music to date. The ruling essentially shut down Napster in its former incarnation and set the stage for future law-driven clamp-downs on P2P distribution of media online.

As we discussed earlier, Napster was the world's first large scale peer-to-peer file sharing service, meaning that the service enabled users to search the hard drives of other users connected to the service, and connect with one another to share files. Sued by A&M and other record labels assisted by the RIAA, Napster argued in court that since they were not actually providing the copyrighted files, but rather just enabling communication among users, the company could not be held liable for copyright infringement because they fall under the "service provider" exception of the DMCA, discussed in chapter 9. Napster also presented the defense of fair use, based on the theories that (i) the service also enabled the sharing of authorized music from new artists, (ii) sampling, and (iii) "space-shifting," a defense used by Sony in the landmark Betamax case in the 1980s.

Napster lost in district court, where Judge Marilyn Patel stated that:

> *Although downloading and uploading MP3 music files is not paradigmatic commercial activity, it is also not personal use in the traditional sense. Plaintiffs have not shown that the majority of Napster users download music to sell—that is, for profit. However, given the vast scale of Napster use among anonymous individuals, the court finds that downloading and uploading MP3 music files with the assistance of Napster are not private uses. At the very least, a host user sending a file cannot be said to engage in a personal use when distributing that file to an anonymous requester. Moreover, the fact that Napster users get for free something they would ordinarily have to buy suggests that they reap economic advantages from Napster use.*[3]

Napster appealed the decision to the Ninth Circuit Court of Appeals, where they lost yet again, resulting in an injunction

---

3 A&M Records, Inc. v. Napster, Inc., 114 F. Supp. 2d 896 (N.D. Cal. 2000).

requiring Napster to remove all copyrighted material from the service. The injunction led to the shutdown of the Napster service in its former incarnation because the company did not have the technology to filter files and comply with the injunction. At the time, Napster had a verified user base of over 25 million people.

A&M RECORDS, INC. V. NAPSTER, 239 F.3D 1004, (9TH CIR. 2001)

Numerous guiding principles were derived from the Ninth Circuit opinion, including the following three particularly relevant guidelines:

1. The free, unlicensed downloading of a complete audio file as a "sample" does not qualify for a fair use defense.

   The record supports a finding that free promotional downloads are highly regulated by the record company plaintiffs and that the companies collect royalties for song samples available on retail Internet sites. . . .

   The district court further found that both the market for audio CDs and market for online distribution are adversely affected by Napster's service . . . the court did not abuse its discretion when it found that, overall, Napster has an adverse impact on the audio CD and digital download markets. The record supports the district court's preliminary determinations that: (1) the more music that sampling users download, the less likely they are to eventually purchase the recordings on audio CD; and (2) even if the audio CD market is not harmed, Napster has adverse effects on the developing digital download market.[4]

2. Napster's space-shifting is not fair use. Space-shifting—the practice of downloading an MP3 file of a track already owned on a CD for listening elsewhere—was yet another feature of the Napster service that was deemed not eligible for a fair use defense—a defense that had been successfully applied to other contexts (such as VHS videotapes).

   It is obvious that once a user lists a copy of music he already owns on the Napster system in order to access the music from another location, the song becomes "available to millions of other individuals," not just the original CD owner.[5]

---

4   A&M Records, Inc. v. Napster, 239 F.3d 1004, (9th Cir. 2001)
5   A&M Records, Inc. v. Napster, 239 F.3d 1004, (9th Cir. 2001)

3. A distributor can be held to be a "vicarious infringer" for failure to
    control or stop infringing activities when they are financially benefiting
    and have the ability to supervise, but do not do so. Because Napster
    failed to actively police their users, the company could be held liable
    for vicarious infringement.

*In the context of copyright law, vicarious liability extends beyond
an employer/employee relationship to cases in which a defendant
"has the right and ability to supervise the infringing activity and also
has a direct financial interest in such activities.... Financial benefit
exists where the availability of infringing material 'acts as a draw for
customers....' Napster's future revenue is directly dependent upon
'increases in userbase.' Here, plaintiffs have demonstrated that
Napster retains the right to control access to its system. Napster has
an express reservation of rights policy, stating on its Web site that it
expressly reserves the 'right to refuse service and terminate accounts
in [its] discretion, including, but not limited to, if Napster believes that
user conduct violates applicable law ... or for any reason in Napster's
sole discretion, with or without cause.' To escape imposition of
vicarious liability, the reserved right to police must be exercised to its
fullest extent. Turning a blind eye to detectable acts of infringement for
the sake of profit gives rise to liability."* [6]

See appendix C for a longer excerpt of this case.

METRO-GOLDWYN-MAYER STUDIOS INC., ET AL. V.
GROKSTER, LTD., 545 U.S. 913 (2005)

Four years after Napster, in yet another very notable ruling on copyright and music law, the U.S. Supreme Court in 2005 heard the case
of Metro-Goldwyn-Mayer Studios Inc., et al. v. Grokster, Ltd. (Note
that the Napster case went only to U.S. Court of Appeals for the
Ninth Circuit, and was not decided by the Supreme Court.)

The facts leading up to the case were quite simple: the defendants (Grokster and StreamCast) distributed free software products
that allowed computer users to share electronic files through P2P
networks. The Grokster and StreamCast (Morpheus) products were

---

6   A&M Records, Inc. v. Napster, 239 F.3d 1004, (9th Cir. 2001)

slightly different from the original Napster, in that their products merely enabled users to search the computers of other users. The products were cleverly designed so that at no point was the search communication processed by any of the defendants' products.

Recognizing the similarity in use and functionality, a collective of copyright holders (MGM, with other motion picture studios, recording companies, songwriters, and music publishers) sued Grokster and StreamCast for their users' copyright infringements. Their claim was that the defendants knowingly and intentionally distributed their software products to enable users to reproduce and distribute copyrighted works in violation of basic copyright law.

The question addressed by the Court was "under what circumstances the distributor of a product capable of both lawful and unlawful use is liable for the acts of copyright infringement by third parties using the product." The Court held that those who distribute and promote an object that fosters infringement can be held liable for the infringing acts of its users (third parties):

> ... that one who distributes a device with the object of promoting its use to infringe copyright, as shown by clear expression or other affirmative steps taken to foster infringement, is liable for the resulting acts of infringement by third parties.[7]

The case is of interest for numerous reasons. For one, the intent behind the development of a music distribution product and whether its users' actions are monitored can define whether it is a legal one. As stated by the Court:

> Grokster and StreamCast are not, however, merely passive recipients of information about infringing use. The record is replete with evidence that from the moment Grokster and StreamCast began to distribute their free software, each one clearly voiced the objective that recipients use it to download copyrighted works, and each took active steps to encourage infringement.[8]

Evidence had been introduced at trial showing that the companies actively promoted the illegal uses of their product. Further:

> Finally, there is no evidence that either company made an effort to filter copyrighted material from users' downloads or otherwise

---

7   Metro-Goldwyn-Mayer Studios Inc., Et Al. v. Grokster, Ltd., 545 U.S. 913 (2005)
8   Metro-Goldwyn-Mayer Studios Inc., Et Al. v. Grokster, Ltd., 545 U.S. 913 (2005)

impede the sharing of copyrighted files. Although Grokster appears to have sent e-mails warning users about infringing content when it received threatening notice from the copyright holders, it never blocked anyone from continuing to use its software to share copyrighted files. StreamCast not only rejected another company's offer of help to monitor infringement, but blocked the Internet Protocol addresses of entities it believed were trying to engage in such monitoring on its networks ...[9]

Summing up their decision, the Court stated:

[O]ne who distributes a device with the object of promoting its use to infringe copyright, as shown by clear expression or other affirmative steps taken to foster infringement, is liable for the resulting acts of infringement by third parties.[10]

And with that, the Supreme Court of the United States attempted to further control the availability of products that can be (and are primarily used) for infringing purposes.

See appendix D for a longer excerpt of this case.

SECTION 115 REFORM

Another major gap in copyright administration for the digital music business in the United States is the lack of a central clearinghouse for music publishing. Although the mechanical royalty rates for interactive streaming appear to have been set, there are limited options available to legitimate digital music services that want to obtain the requisite mechanical licenses without going to each individual publisher. Further complicating matters, centralized licensing options aside, the initial and most urgent problem lies in the lack of a centralized database or other location where potential licensees—in many cases, companies that are willing to enter into a license and pay a fee—can simply go to locate the rights holders with the power to license use of compositions. While there is a push among publishers, distributors, and other interested parties to collaborate towards this end, efforts have yet to bear fruit, in part due to such deeply conflicting interests and disagreements over funding and ownership, despite a common goal. This has resulted

---

9   Metro-Goldwyn-Mayer Studios Inc., Et Al. v. Grokster, Ltd., 545 U.S. 913 (2005)
10   Metro-Goldwyn-Mayer Studios Inc., Et Al. v. Grokster, Ltd., 545 U.S. 913 (2005)

in relatively high licensing costs and extreme inefficiency for the companies legally offering these products.

DIFFICULTIES, GENERALLY

On a larger scale, copyright law has encountered extreme difficulty responding adequately to online piracy. Policing the Internet and punishing millions of individuals who share files with one another is a close to impossible task. How can Congress protect the value of works, when that value has already been diminished by their unobstructed and free availability on P2P sites? A select number of artists are already giving up, making their music available for free on the theory that the liberal availability of their sound recordings will increase other streams of revenue. Labels operate with intense fear that a new song or album will be leaked online before the official release date, thus greatly reducing its value when finally officially made available through legitimate sources.

This is perhaps the greatest issue facing copyright law today.

CHAPTER 9

DMCA/Copyright Law Reform

As we have discussed, the Digital Millennium Copyright Act ("DMCA") was signed into law by Bill Clinton in 1998. Among other things, the DMCA serves two primary purposes: (1) it extends the reach of copyright law in the digital age, and (2) it limits the liability of the providers of online services for copyright infringement by their users. The law, meant to bring U.S. law into compliance with the World Intellectual Property Organization ("WIPO") treaties, criminalized the production and dissemination of technology, devices, or services intended to circumvent measures that control access to copyrighted works (i.e., digital rights management or "DRM"), as well as the act of actually circumventing an access control, such as tampering with a digital fingerprint. The law makes such activities criminal whether or not there is actual infringement of copyright itself.

To limit liability of service providers, the DMCA sets forth certain guidelines that if followed, relieve such providers of legal exposure and risk associated with their otherwise innocent delivery of infringing works.

For example, the DMCA provides a "safe harbor" for ISPs, stating that service providers who merely provide a gateway to the Internet (e.g., AT&T or Comcast) cannot be held liable for the infringing acts of their customers/users. However, the limited liability of ISPs exists only in cases where the ISP meets certain conditions including giving the infringing end-users warnings that what they are doing is wrong and terminating repeat offenders. (It was this safe harbor provision that the original Napster tried to hide behind in its 2000–2001 battle with record labels, which we addressed in chapter 8).

Under the DMCA, a "safe harbor" also exists for services such as YouTube who might actually store infringing material, if they meet the following requirements:

1. They do not receive a financial benefit directly attributable to the infringing activity,
2. They are not aware of the presence of infringing material or know any facts or circumstances that would make infringing material apparent, and
3. Upon receiving notice from copyright owners or their agents, they act expeditiously to remove the purported infringing material.

ISPs, however, have been working with the music industry to cut piracy under the DMCA, sometimes involuntarily. As part of its enforcement efforts against piracy, the RIAA in 2003 began filing civil lawsuits against individuals who illegally traded music online. In order to identify such users, the RIAA needed data from ISPs, and served the service providers with subpoenas under the DMCA demanding the identity of users tied to Internet Protocol (IP) addresses known to be used in sharing music online.

For example, the RIAA used the subpoena power in section 512(h) of the DMCA to request the identity of Verizon Internet users who were thought to be involved in piracy via P2P networks. In this case, Verizon refused to comply with the RIAA order, arguing that the Verizon network did not actually store the material but instead merely transmitted it. Verizon ultimately lost the case, and the RIAA has sued over two thousand individuals for copyright infringement. The vast majority of the cases against individual file-sharers were settled out of court, but at least two cases went to trial and resulted in large monetary awards against the infringers.

The DMCA has remained the subject of great debate and in recent years, high profile litigation. For example, at the time of press, we are still awaiting the outcome of the well publicized and high stakes infringement case initiated by Viacom Inc. against YouTube (Google Inc.) for the alleged unauthorized distribution of 160,000 videos on Google's YouTube site. In the ongoing case, the ability of Google to present a fair use and DMCA safe harbor defense is at question. The stakes are high. The initial claim demanded one billion dollars in statutory damages.

Separately, in IO Group Inc. v. Veoh Networks Inc., a case with similar facts, the U.S. District Court for the Northern District of California ruled that the defendant Veoh qualified for protection under the safe harbor of the DMCA. Veoh had made it clear that it regarded copyright infringement as a serious matter by responding to DMCA takedown notices within 24 hours, registering a Copyright Agent with the Copyright Office, providing warnings to users about infringement, and terminating repeat infringers. Many believe that the law can and should be credited with the concentration of highly successful online distribution companies in the United States. Regardless of what one thinks of it, the DMCA remains a powerful piece of legislation in the United States—a law that shapes much of online media distribution generally.

So, what does the DMCA have to do with music law? A lot. Depending on where one falls in the digital music distribution food chain from creator to consumer, the DMCA largely shapes the way music is distributed online, and why. The law also creates a standard for starting an Internet radio station, as discussed in chapter 7. We will give examples of its application to each of the primary players in this distribution chain.

THE DMCA AND THE MUSIC BUSINESS

There are numerous ways that the DMCA could come into play in the digital music industry; we will focus on three primary examples in a Q&A format: (1) an artist who finds her work available via an online music store without any knowledge of how it got there, (2) an independent record label that has licensed its catalog to an ad-supported streaming service only to find that the service won't distribute half of it "due to DMCA takedowns from a music publisher," and (3) a digital distributor that receives dozens of demands for removal of content weekly.

HOW DO I USE THE DMCA TO REMOVE MY CONTENT FROM A WEB SITE?

I recorded a solo album three years ago. I sold several thousand copies on tour, via my own Web site (linked from my MySpace page) and other online sources. I never signed with a record label or licensed this album for any online distribution, but I am considering doing so in the future. Last week, I found this album for sale on two major online music stores. What should I do to have it removed?

Answer: *The DMCA will provide complete guidance on how to proceed, but the first step is to look at the distributor Web site's Terms of Service or Terms of Use, typically found via a link on one of the first pages of the web store.*

Find the name and address of the store's designated "Copyright Agent" and send them what is known in the industry as a "DMCA Takedown Notice" (see chapter 12 for a sample takedown notice). A takedown notice must be in writing and must include:

1. *the physical or electronic signature of the one asserting the right to takedown,*
2. *identification of the work allegedly infringed,*
3. *identification of the allegedly infringing material sufficiently to permit the distributor to find, remove, and/or limit access,*
4. *the sender's contact information,*
5. *a statement that the complaining party has a good faith belief that use of the material is not authorized, and*
6. *a statement that the information in the notice is accurate and, under penalty of perjury, that either the owner or the complaining party is authorized to act on behalf of the owner of an exclusive right that is allegedly infringed.[1]*

Once the distributor company has received a proper DMCA takedown notice that satisfies these six requirements, they must remove the content until further notice. It is then up to you to work with the distributor or the original licensor to obtain an accounting and/or reporting information about prior distribution and associated royalties, if any. Depending on the nature of the parties, this process could take some time in part because governing license agreements typically contain confidentiality commitments, indemnification provisions, and other limitations on sharing of such information.

Alternatively, you could pursue a license with the distributing entity so that instead of taking the content down, they start to pay you the royalties attributable to the distribution of the work. This can be achieved by requesting licensing information rather than a takedown. Note that this same analysis applies to on demand streams in addition to downloads; both require a license and can be removed for lack thereof.

WHAT ABOUT THE INTERPLAY BETWEEN PUBLISHERS AND RECORD LABELS IN A DMCA WORLD?

I own a mid-size independent record label with about five hundred signed artists. We recently did a distribution deal with a popular ad-supported streaming service only to find that the service won't distribute half of it "due to DMCA takedowns from a music publisher." What does this mean?

---

1   17 U.S.C. § 52(c)(3)

Answer: *This means that a music publisher claiming rights in the underlying compositions to that portion of your catalog has sent a takedown notice, as we discussed above, to the service and that the service has complied. If you want the catalog reinstated on the service, your best bet is to contact the music publisher and see if you can work together to come to an agreement on acceptable license terms.*

WHAT DOES THE DMCA HAVE TO DO WITH SUBLICENSING ONLINE?

I run the content operations division of a niche digital music service. Every week, we receive dozens of e-mails from artists, labels, heirs to artists, and others saying that they did not give us permission to make content that they own available on our service. I have had our licensing attorney check the source of the allegedly unlicensed content, and it turns out that in 99 percent of cases, the content is in fact licensed to us by a label or aggregator (with associated publishing rights cleared as well). What should I do? I don't want to take content down that should be up, but I also don't want the company to be subject to copyright infringement risk.

Answer: *You are right to be concerned about this. The DMCA, however, puts the burden of managing copyright on the owners of such copyrights, and the law includes specific terms around how rights holders can assert such rights. ("The DMCA notification procedures place the burden of policing copyright infringement—identifying the potentially infringing material and adequately documenting the infringement—squarely on the owners of the copyright.")[2] In such a situation, it is nearly impossible for a distributor to know if the licensor of the content or the author of these demands for removal is the true owner of the associated copyright(s). A good first step in response to these notices is to review them all for compliance with the six-part takedown guidelines as set forth in section 512 of the Act. If the notices comply with the DMCA, you should take the content down until you can determine who is right. If they don't comply with the DMCA takedown guidelines (for example, they simply say that the use was not authorized), you can respond to the sender with a request for a DMCA compliant notice with a reference to your posted DMCA takedown policy (that you should definitely have, if you don't already). Often, the sixth component—requiring a statement under penalty of perjury that the sender has the right to the content and to demand its removal—will serve as an effective filter and will limit these notices to the legitimate ones. (You should*

---

2   Perfect 10 v CCBill, 488 F.3d 1102, 1113 (9th Cir. 2007)

also check your contracts with your sublicensor to ensure they indemnify you in the event they provide you infringing material.)

WHAT ABOUT RIGHTS IN DIFFERENT TERRITORIES?

Why don't DMCA takedown notices require that the complainants specify the territory in which they want the content removed?

Answer: *Some record labels and other licensors have rights on a territory-by-territory basis and may be able to demand takedown in the United States, but not Canada. Surprisingly, the DMCA is silent on territory. We can't tell you if this was a deliberate move or an accident. Until this is clarified, perhaps in a future amendment, the parties need to work together to ensure that takedowns are done in a manner that is the best for all parties involved, from both a legal and a business standpoint. This might mean tailoring takedowns to the specific demands of the sender and possibly even doing research to determine a licensor's territory rights.*

These are just a few examples of how the DMCA comes into play in the music industry. Though the law is often criticized for making it too easy for distributors to simply remove content as a protective measure, it has served numerous other purposes fairly well and will continue to shape the way distributors and rights holders manage content online.

WHAT IS A DMCA "SAFE HARBOR?"

Title II of the DMCA, the Online Copyright Infringement Liability Limitation Act ("OCILLA"), creates what is known as a "safe harbor"—essentially, limitations on liability for monetary relief for some service providers. To qualify, ISPs must comply with certain prescribed safe harbor guidelines and promptly block access to allegedly infringing material if they receive a DMCA compliant notice. Such guidelines include: (1) adherence to a policy for the termination of service for repeat infringers, (2) accommodation of and noninterference with technical measures used to protect against infringement, (3) designation of a Copyright Agent, and (4) compliance with reasonably alleged takedown notices. In turn, an ISP can lose its safe harbor eligibility for the safe harbor if it (a) has actual or "red flag" knowledge of infringing activity on the service, and (b) "receive[s] a financial benefit directly attributable to the infringing activity, in a case in which the service provider has the right and ability to control such activity."[3]

SO, WHAT DOES THE FUTURE HOLD?

Copyright law will continue to be stretched to accommodate innovation, and it is sure to continue to be painful for most of the stakeholders in the industries affected. What can we expect to see in future years? Where do successful business models lie? Who will be the industry's successful players in 2014? 2030? Will conflict among licensors give way to collaboration for the greater good? These are all questions that are soon to be answered, many in surprising ways in months and years to come. Here are some ideas regarding what we should expect.

ISPs WILL BE INCREASINGLY INVOLVED WITH ENFORCEMENT OF INTELLECTUAL PROPERTY LAWS

At long last, at least from the perspective of the copyright owners, ISPs finally appear to be playing a role in enforcement of intellectual property laws. Numerous countries, including France, Australia, and the United States, are seeing the emergence of new guidelines—both privately agreed to between trade organizations and public companies (RIAA, AT&T, Comcast) and publicly imposed via legislation (for example, France's new ISP enforcement laws, which were held unconstitutional by a French court in June 2009). Several European ISPs have agreed to a three-strikes provision with the music industry, in essence agreeing to take away Internet access from those who are caught pirating copyrighted material three times. Perhaps it is true that fear of having one's Internet service suspended is a greater concern than being caught and pursued via the legal system. It certainly can have a more immediate impact on the infringer.

---

3   17 U.S.C. § 512(c)(1)(B); § 512(d)(2)

Such guidelines serve to impose some responsibility on service providers to create and enforce policies with regard to infringement that takes place via their services. While ISPs are effectively free of liability if they satisfy the safe-harbor provisions of the DMCA, there are commercial reasons to cooperate with such new demands on the part of powerful rights holders (record labels, collecting societies, etc.). In some cases, content providers want to partner with ISPs to roll out new offerings, and there is potential new revenue associated with a multi-part arrangement pursuant to which ISPs collect an additional fee for the service that is used to cover certain content license fees for distribution of media via such a service. Further, cooperation could serve to befriend potential litigants. One thing seems already to be apparent: ISP customers are more likely to stop infringing activity via the threat of loss of Internet connectivity than a remote threat of arrest for copyright infringement.

Access Models Are Likely to Continue to Grow in Popularity

As Internet access becomes more and more pervasive and we approach a time where unlimited and uninterrupted WiFi access is not limited to metropolitan areas, consumers are more likely to use access-based services to obtain their music than the traditional purchase model. Over-the-air downloads are now available on Apple iPhones and other devices, meaning you can download music from the iTunes store and listen on your iPhone's iPod software from anywhere you receive wireless service. Like many evolutions in industry, this one turns on technology and infrastructure. For artists and other licensors, this means that it is important to ensure that any outbound license agreements have terms that will adapt well to increased access-based distribution so as not to be left out of such revenue streams.

Blanket Licenses

Others have argued that perhaps an ISP flat fee is the best way to collect revenue lost to piracy. As of 2009, the RIAA is experimenting with blanket licenses on college campuses through a program called Choruss. Staffed by Warner Music consultants, the company hopes to implement unlimited access to music for students at colleges that are part of the program, paid for through an increased student activity fee.

The role ISPs play in the distribution of music and other media will no doubt be an interesting area to watch in coming months and years.

CREATIVE COMMONS AND THE "COPYLEFT" MOVEMENT

While Congress and entertainment industry professionals argue about the best way to protect works, there are some on the other end of the spectrum who argue that the solution is to limit copyright protection. One of the leaders of this "copyleft" movement is former Stanford and current Harvard law professor Lawrence Lessig.

Fig. 9.1. The Copyleft Symbol

Lessig, the founder and former CEO of Creative Commons, has become the face and name of what is known as the copyleft movement. Together with the Creative Commons organization, he has successfully managed to break ground in establishing a new approach to copyright where creative works are more available to others to build new works upon. The heart of this idea lies in the "Creative Commons licenses," innovative licenses that allow for the creator to determine and communicate what exclusive rights they preserve and what exclusive rights they waive in releasing their creations to the public.

As an example, consider the following. The band Nine Inch Nails released *Ghost I–IV* in 2008, a collection of thirty-six instrumental tracks licensed under a Creative Commons license that allowed users to remix and share the tracks with anyone, as long as they were not for commercial gain. Some thought this was innovative for it supported wide dissemination of the content, created buzz around the album, and actually seems to have encouraged sales. Some thought it was foolish for it supported the notion of "free" music and could subject the artist to a dramatic reduction in revenues stemming from album sales. Either way, it is an example of a new approach gaining traction in a new era of copyright.

In his commentary on piracy, Lessig points to a failed system of tracking copies on the Internet that could one day be changed with the advent of successful controlled access systems.

"Sales might go up, my reputation might go up (or down), but there is no way to trace the drop in sales to this individual theft, and no way to link the rise (or fall) in fame to this subsidized distribution.... So a system that controlled access in this more fine-grained way would grant access to its resources only to another system that controlled access in the same fine-grained way. A hierarchy of systems would develop; and copyright material would be traded only within that system that controlled access properly."[4]

As Lessig points out in his book *Code: Version 2.0,* "An important point about copyright law is that, though designed in part to protect authors, the control it was designed to create was never meant to be perfect."[5] Fair use exceptions and other limited terms mean that copyright is not an all-encompassing absolute right of an author. Consumers may also sell their copy of a book or CD, without payment of a royalty, under the first sale doctrine.

Lessig also made waves a few years ago when he suggested an "alternative compensation scheme," a tax to be levied at the ISP level on every consumer to help the shortfall in revenue due to piracy—one of the very systems now being considered. Payments could be calculated by tracking the traffic of music on the Internet via an embedded watermark placed by copyright holders into DRM-free music files, or other tracing mechanisms.

The owner of the copyright in an audio or video recording who wished to be compensated when it was used by others would register it with the Copyright Office and would receive, in return, a unique file name, which then would be used to track its distribution, consumption, and modification. The government would raise the money necessary to compensate copyright owners through a tax most likely, a tax on the devices and services that consumers use to gain access to digital entertainment. Using techniques pioneered by television rating

---

4   "The Law of the Horse: What Cyberlaw Might Teach." *Harvard Law Review.* 113: (1999), 501

5   Lessig, Lawrence. *Code: Version 2.0.* New York: Basic, 2006

services and performing rights organizations, a government agency would estimate the frequency with which each song and film was listened to or watched. The tax revenues would then be distributed to copyright owners in proportion to the rates with which their registered works were being consumed."[6]

While the idea is interesting, implementation of such a major change in revenue structure will no doubt require years for debate, study of the impact, passage of legislation, and implementation of the technological systems. And while the copyleft movement has received a great deal of publicity, it is opposed by many creators and industry organizations alike, although some parts of its plans may indeed come to fruition.

HOW MUCH DOES GLOBAL INTERNET PIRACY COST THE SOUND RECORDING INDUSTRY?

Analysis by the Institute for Policy Innovation concludes that global sound recording piracy causes:

- $12.5 billion in economic losses every year
- 71,060 U.S. jobs lost (of this amount, 26,860 jobs would have been added in the sound recording industry or in downstream retail industries, while 44,200 jobs would have been added in other U.S. industries)
- Loss of $2.7 billion in worker's earning (of this total, $1.1 billion would have been earned by workers in the sound recording industry or in downstream retail industries while $1.6 billion would have been earned by workers in other U.S. industries)
- Loss of $422 million in tax revenues
- Loss of $291 million in personal income tax
- Loss of $131 million in corporate income and production taxes[7]

---

6 http://lessig.org/blog/2004/10/alternative_compensation_syste.html
7 www.narm.com/2008Conv/StateoftheIndustry.pdf

Web 2.0: How Virtual Worlds, Social Networking Sites, Advertisers, Bloggers, and Others Fit In

What is "Web 2.0" and what does it have to do with music? The term "Web 2.0" appears on its face to refer to a new version of the World Wide Web when in fact it merely applies to new uses thereof. Specifically, Web 2.0 refers to new uses of the Internet—uses that leverage use of applications in a collaborative manner. Examples of Web 2.0 applications include social networking, Wikipedia, blogs, open-source applications, user-generated and user-posted content sites, and others.

To a copyleft opponent, the Web 2.0 generation of sites and services pose a whole new level of threat to conventional copyright protection. Now, not only can music (and any other copyrighted content) be copied and easily sent among users online, but users can post content to their own personal sites or pages, or on heavily trafficked user-generated content or "UGC" sites. By definition, Web 2.0 sites allow users to build upon and interact with information or content, and often that means third-party owned music content. Perhaps the largest examples of these are YouTube and MySpace, which have negotiated blanket licenses with some record labels and publishers to cover the widespread use of their music on the sites.

So, are there different copyright rules that apply to such uses? Do users who post a song on their blog need a license from the rights holder(s)? Does the background music on my personal social networking page need to be licensed? The answer to these questions is yes, if the person posting the materials does not legally control the content. That said, there are still several to-be-answered questions in this area with case law and practice currently defining what is legal and acceptable.

WHAT CAN I POST TO YOUTUBE?

I have a video of my daughter lip-synching a popular hip-hop song. Can I post this to YouTube without infringing anyone's copyright?

Answer: *Not necessarily. As was played out in the Lenz v. Universal case in the Northern District of California, there remain numerous unanswered questions with regard to copyright and the Web 2.0 era. The Lenz case came about when a mother posted a 29-second video of her child dancing to "Let's Go Crazy," a song recorded by Prince, the sound recording of which is licensed by Universal Records. Universal requested and obtained a takedown from YouTube, which was followed by the video being reposted by YouTube at Lenz's request using the little-used portion of the DMCA codified at 17 U.S.C. § 512(g)(3) (counter-notification pursuant to which the original poster states under penalty of perjury that they have "a good faith belief that the material was removed or disabled as a result of mistake or misidentification of the material to be removed or disabled"). Essentially, Lenz had sent YouTube a DMCA counter-notification taking the position that her video constituted a "fair use" of "Let's Go Crazy" and thus did not infringe any third party copyrights. The video was reposted by YouTube after which Lenz utilized an even more rarely employed portion of the DMCA, 17 U.S.C. § 512(f), which provides for liability upon those who file DMCA notices without the requisite good faith belief that the material in question is an infringement of the copyright owner's rights. Universal's subsequent motion to dismiss was denied, setting some powerful precedent for those tinkering in the Web 2.0 space. In a nutshell, rights holders issuing takedown notices have a duty to consider whether a use is a "fair use" just as much as a poster has a duty to consider whether a use is legal.*

One's perception of Web 2.0 likely turns on whether one is a subscriber to the copyright or the copyleft movement. For the music industry, this next generation of uses of the Internet spells increased opportunity for exposure and distribution alongside increased risk of economic loss. For optimists, the Web 2.0 era is shining a bright light on one area of copyright law that could likely benefit from reform. Perhaps it will be the increased prevalence of Web 2.0 applications that will force the industry into a collectively agreed upon blanket license for noncommercial uses. Perhaps Creative Commons licenses will become more mainstream. No matter what, the rights of the original creators and those seeking to reuse or repurpose third party works are going to continue to need to be balanced against one another in Congress, the courts, and online.

In the meantime, rights holders and others in the music industry should be viewing and treating Web 2.0 uses of musical content the same way one would treat other uses: it should be licensed or fall into a license exception (fair use, for example), or it cannot be legally used. There is currently no outright exception to copyright law for non-commercial uses; so whether music is posted on a private blog with three viewers or a popular UGC gaming site, copyright implications need to be carefully considered. Further, there is no blanket or wholesale licensing system available for such Web 2.0 uses, so each use and each distinct piece of content is subject to its own copyright clearance or infringement analysis. The hope for many in the industry is that this will change with time, but to date, the law is moving slowly, and many believe that substantial change in business standards can only occur as a result of government intervention. Regardless of where one falls on the copyright/copyleft spectrum, the emergence of these new uses of the Internet is going to further challenge copyright law as we know it in months and years to come.

WHO PAYS IF I UPLOAD TO MYSPACE?

Wanton Success has covered a Johnny Cash tune, and wants to post the song on their MySpace page. Under the compulsory license scheme, Wanton Success is entitled to a mechanical license at the statutory rate, as we discussed earlier. But is posting for streaming legal? Who pays the public performance and mechanical royalties for this, if MySpace is a free offering for artists?

Answer: *This is a thorny area. Theoretically, a stream includes both a mechanical and a public performance component. Mechanicals should be paid by the service under the CRB rates set in the fall of 2008 for streaming, and MySpace should have licenses in place with the PROs to cover the public performance of works. However, MySpace specifically requires users to certify that they are only uploading content they control. The site's terms of service also state that users warrant that content they upload does not violate the rights of a third party and that the user is responsible for the payment of royalties. (This is why you should always read the terms of service when joining an online service, even though most people just click "agree" and move on without a second thought.)*

So, in this case, unless Wanton Success has specifically cleared the use with Johnny (or the song's current owner) or obtained assurance that MySpace will take responsibility for the licensing, Wanton Success should steer clear of uploading their version of the song to MySpace.

CHAPTER 11

International
Considerations

This book is focused on United States music and copyright law. While there are certainly some themes that cross borders (the fundamental copyright law basics, for example), applicable law and business practices vary widely from territory to territory. The way music is licensed for public performance, and the right of sound recording copyright holders to receive royalties for radio play, for example, are significantly different overseas.

Copyright provides exclusive rights to authors (or their assignees) and protects creative works. But how can copyright work successfully on a global scale in our "digital age" when each country has its own laws? What are the various stakeholders in the music distribution chain to do in an effort to properly manage these multiple variables? Whether you are an artist, a distributor, or one of the founders of a budding startup, if you plan to cross borders, you are best advised to seek professional consultation along the way. Requirements from country to country—as well as ownership rights—may vary greatly. With infringement and investment stakes as high as they are, it is wise to be as informed as possible when working in unfamiliar territories.

As we mentioned briefly in chapter 3, some international treaties may provide copyright protection for creative works abroad.

Berne Convention

Perhaps the most important international copyright treaty is the Berne Convention, which resulted from an international agreement first accepted in 1886 at Berne, Switzerland. In short, the treaty provides that an author of a work is entitled to the same protections as a domestic author in any country that is a signatory to the Convention. The treaty has 164 members, but despite its widespread acceptance, the United States did not become an official party to the Berne Convention until 103 years later in 1989. Although the copyright law of the country will apply whenever a claim is applied, *in no event will the duration of copyright protection extend beyond whatever it would be in the author's home country* (known as the "rule of the shorter term").

Geneva Convention

Equally important to our discussion of international copyright and music is the Geneva Convention, which specifically requires each signatory to protect authors of "phonograms" (i.e., sound recordings) against the making, importation, or distribution of duplicates of their works without permission. The United States became a member of the Geneva Convention in 1974.

Rome Convention

The 1963 Rome Convention established certain protections that were meant to extend beyond those created by the Berne Convention in response to new technologies. In general, performers (actors, singers, musicians, dancers, and other persons who perform literary or artistic works), producers, and broadcasters are protected against the broadcasting and the communication to the public of their live performance, the fixation of their live performance, and the reproduction of such a fixation if they have not explicitly consented. The United States is not yet a signatory to the Rome Convention.

Smaller Treaties

Finally, other smaller treaties such as the Buenos Aires Convention also exist. The Buenos Aires Convention provides for mutual recognition of copyrights in countries in Latin America and the United States. At this time, however, all parties to the Buenos Aires Convention are also parties to the Berne Convention.

Clearing Rights in Multiple Territories

Translating rights across borders comes with its own challenges. In Europe, the advent of the European Union and the continued push to standardize business across the continent has raised the issue of pan-European licensing for public performance of compositions. Rather than having multiple representatives and dealing with a PRO in each country, music rights holders are pushing to offer one-stop shopping for those who want to license their music for use across Europe. For instance, in January 2008, Warner/Chappell Music, the publishing arm of Warner Music Group, and one of the world's largest music publishers, revealed the first three collecting societies to sign up for Warner's new Pan-European Digital Licensing (PEDL) initiative. Those three societies are GEMA, the MCPS-PRS Alliance, and STIM (see appendix A). The PEDL initiative simplifies the process for rights users licensing Warner/Chappell's catalogue, and grants non-exclusive rights in the catalogue to those collecting societies that comply with a set of common standards intended to ensure the efficient, transparent management of rights as well as appropriate and accurate compensation for songwriters.

Separately, CELAS is a society specifically created to clear pan-European licenses. A joint venture between PRS and GELA, and operating out of offices in the UK and Germany, CELAS has the exclusive rights to blanket license the EMI Publishing catalogue across Europe.

Due to worldwide nature of the Internet, online music sites face their own range of challenges in ensuring that they comply with licensor-mandated territory restrictions. Some sites, such as iTunes, control access and licensing based on the IP address of the user or the address associated with a customer's credit card. However, illegitimate sites such as Pirate Bay and torrent sites generally do not seek to limit access on a territory-by-territory basis (for obvious reasons). Anybody with an interest in learning more about music law outside of the United States is encouraged to pursue research on a territory-by-territory basis. As a good starting point, we have compiled a list of the international collecting societies and other international resources in appendix B.

CHAPTER 12

How to Start an
Online Music Service

There are a range of considerations associated with starting a company that will legally distribute music via the Internet. We'll leave the fundamentals (funding, product offering, etc.) to the empowered leaders and venture capitalists. From a licensing standpoint, the following are the steps one needs to take.

The market has revealed two primary ways to launch an online service that includes music: the legitimate, legal, and costly way and the immediate, risky, and illegal way. Naturally, there are a number of success stories associated with each, but we do not advise or support anything other than a legal, legitimate approach to distributing copyrighted works, despite associated expense and hassle. While some may disagree, the problems and challenges faced in launching a new service will only persist if the business community is anything less than motivated to support positive change.

The immediate, risky, and illegal way to launch a service that includes music is to just do it without any (or at least without all) required licenses. This is the "ask for forgiveness, not permission" tactic employed by a number of services launched in the past decade, including LyricFind and YouTube. While it does not always work, the idea has proven fruitful in a few cases. The approach entails launching an offering and obtaining interest and traffic to the service to better your negotiating position. The hope is that while the rights holders have enormous leverage in later negotiations, they are not likely to shut the service down and are more interested in coming to deal terms due to the potential revenue opportunity the service presents. In order to proceed with this approach, a company must have little to lose and substantial confidence in their offering; it has to be good enough to generate substantial attention and popularity extremely quickly. Note, however, that for each success story there are hundreds—perhaps thousands—of failures, many of which suffered enormous losses and litigation as a result of their reckless approach to distributing media without requisite licenses in place.

On the other hand, the legitimate, legal, and costly way to launch an online service that includes downloads and streams of music is to obtain all sound recording and composition licenses in advance of making the associated content available. This means getting (1) sound recording licenses for the masters from as many record labels (major and independent) and aggregators as possible, (2) public performance licenses from the PROs (ideally all three in the U.S.: ASCAP, BMI, and SESAC), (3) mechanical licenses from the Harry Fox Agency and any "independent" or "non-HFA" publishers that own compositions underlying the masters you want to distribute, and (4) a license agreement in place with SoundExchange, if you want to include a DMCA compliant radio offering in your service. As one might guess, this process will likely take at least several months and be extremely costly, particularly when you consider legal and other professional fees, associated license fees (including advances), and other costs.

LICENSES REQUIRED

To start a legitimate digital download and online streaming service, one must obtain the following licenses:

1. sound recording licenses from record labels
2. public performance licenses from the PROs
3. mechanical licenses from the Harry Fox Agency and any "independent" publishers
4. sound recording licenses from SoundExchange, if you want to include a DMCA compliant radio offering in your service.

Due to the complicated nature of licensing music, particularly for online distribution, it takes a substantial investment to get into the industry. Some would argue that the convoluted licensing schemes are to blame for a weak catalog of service offerings for legal music. Some even argue that it is understandable that so many services go underground and choose to avoid the legal route altogether. The industry and all involved and invested in it would stand to gain a great deal if we could streamline the process by which a company can launch a legitimate, legal music service for which rights holders are properly paid.

Many argue that the way to go about this is to allow for a more thorough blanket-licensing scheme pursuant to which the quantity of required license agreements would go down due to a centralized clearinghouse mechanism of some kind. While this makes enormous sense, the industry has yet to make any significant progress in that direction. Only time will tell if the cost of properly licensing is so prohibitive that the various stakeholders are forced to compromise for the greater good.

CASH FLOWS IN THE MUSIC INDUSTRY

Musical composition and sound recording copyright holders each have a number of potential revenue streams. In addition, download and subscription services see money flow in from consumers (and advertisers, if the service includes advertisements), and then pay some of such revenues back out to the copyright holders from whom they've licensed the music they make available on their sites. The following charts should give you a better idea of how the money flows.

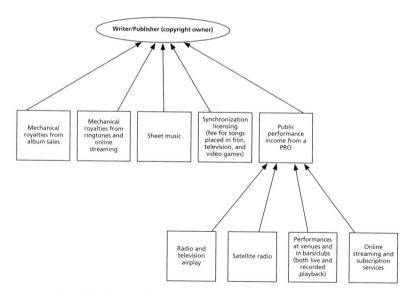

Fig. 12.1. Revenue Streams for a Writer/Music Publisher

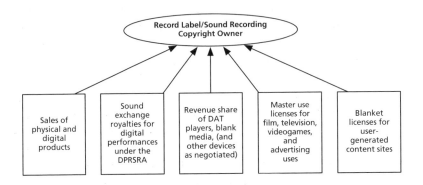

Fig. 12.2. Revenue Streams for a Sound Recording Copyright Holder

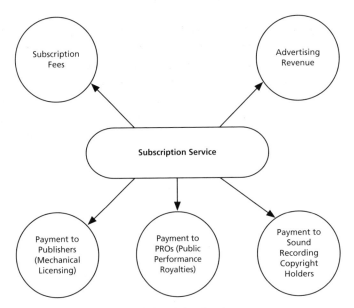

Fig. 12.3. Cash Flows for a Subscription Service

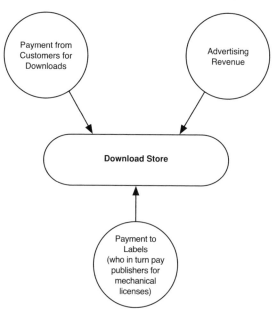

Fig. 12.4. Cash Flows for a Download Service

Artist Checklist

As you probably gather, there is a long list of concerns for copyright holders and creators to consider. If you are an artist, here are a few things to keep in mind:

☐ Register your sound recording copyrights at www.copyright .gov.

☐ Be sure to have assignment of copyright interest from any producers, hired studio musicians, or other persons who worked on your album.

☐ Join a PRO to collect performance royalties on public performances of your work(s).

☐ Make sure you have mechanical licenses in place for any songs you didn't write.

☐ Clear licenses with publishers and labels for any sampling.

☐ For distribution of your music online, content aggregators such as CD Baby, IODA, TuneCore, and The Orchard offer the ability to get your music onto services such as Rhapsody and iTunes without a record label.

☐ Join SoundExchange to receive royalties from digital performances.

☐ Stay on top of any agreements you enter into with labels, promoters, etc. Be aware of termination dates, promotional commitments, your right to leave a label, etc.

Songwriter Checklist

Songwriters also have their share of work to do to ensure they are protected and can earn money from their musical compositions via recording and public performances. If you are a songwriter, here are a few things to keep in mind:

☐ If you co-wrote a song, be sure to talk to your co-writers about the split of copyright ownership, and record your agreement in writing.

☐ Register your musical composition copyrights at www.copyright.gov.

☐ Join a PRO and set up both writer and publisher accounts.

☐ Consider setting up an account with Harry Fox if you want third parties to be able to easily obtain mechanical licenses for your music.

SAMPLE DMCA TAKEDOWN NOTICE

As discussed in chapter 9, a DMCA takedown notice can be sent to online sites demanding removal of materials you believe are infringing. The following is a good example of a DMCA takedown notice:

SAMPLE DMCA TAKEDOWN NOTICE

Date
Company Name
Address
Address

Subject: Notice of Copyright Infringement

I am writing to provide you with a DMCA takedown notice for content appearing on your site. The copyrighted work at issue is the sound recording that appears on www.wheremysongis.com/page.html.

I hereby demand that you immediately remove this content from your site and provide me with an accounting of any and all distributions thereof to date.

You can reach me at via e-mail or phone for further information or clarification. My phone number is +1-202-555-1212. My mailing address is John Doe, 123 Centre Street, Boston, MA 02118.

I have a good faith belief that use of the copyrighted materials described above as allegedly infringing is not authorized by the copyright owner, its agent, or the law, and request that you remove the content.

I swear, under penalty of perjury, that the information in the notification is accurate and that I am the copyright owner or am authorized to act on behalf of the owner of an exclusive right that is allegedly infringed.

Sincerely,

YOUR NAME

Appendices

Abbreviations

ASCAP:	American Society of Composers, Authors, and Publishers
BMI:	Broadcast Music, Inc.
CD:	compact disc
CRB:	Copyright Royalty Board
DAT:	digital audio tape
DMCA:	Digital Millennium Copyright Act
DPD:	digital phonorecord delivery
DPRSRA:	Digital Performance Right in Sound Recording Act
DRM:	digital rights management
EMI:	Electrical and Musical Industries
HFA:	Harry Fox Agency
IFPI:	International Federation of the Phonographic Industry
IP:	Internet protocol or intellectual property
ISP:	Internet service provider
P2P:	peer to peer
PRO:	performing rights organization
RIAA:	Recording Industry Association of America
SESAC:	Society of European Stage Authors and Composers
UMG:	Universal Music Group
WMG:	Warner Music Group

Performing Rights Organizations and Related Companies

UNITED STATES

ASCAP (American Society of Composers, Authors and Publishers)
One Lincoln Plaza
New York, NY 10023
212-621-6000
(Many local offices nationwide)
www.ascap.com

BMI (Broadcast Music, Inc.)
320 W. 57th Street
New York, NY 10019
212-586-2000
(Many local offices nationwide)
www.bmi.com

Harry Fox Agency
601 West 26th Street Suite 500
New York, NY 10001
212-834-0100
www.hfa.com

RIAA (Recording Industry Association of America)
1025 F. Street NW, 10th Floor
Washington, DC 20004
202-775-0101
www.riaa.com

SESAC (Society of European Songwriters and Composers)
55 Music Square East
Nashville, TN 37203
615-320-0055
(Many local offices nationwide)
www.sesac.com

SoundExchange
1121 Fourteenth Street NW, Suite 700
Washington, DC 20005
202-640-5858
www.soundexchange.com

INTERNATIONAL COLLECTING SOCIETIES

United Kingdom

MCPS-PRS Alliance (Mechanical-Copyright Protection Society; PRS addressed separately below)—Exists to collect and pay royalties to its members when their music is recorded and made available to the public (MCPS), and when their music is performed, broadcast, or otherwise made publicly available (PRS For Music)

- Formed in 1997 between two royalty collection societies (MCPS and PRS).
- Money is generated (through license fees) from the recording of members' music on many different formats, including CDs, DVDs, television, broadcast and online.
- Collects for any public performance of music, whether live or recorded, that takes place outside the home and from radio and television broadcasts, and online.
- Ten million pieces of music.
- Member of CISAC.
- www.mcps-prs-alliance.co.uk

PPL (Phonographic Performance Limited)—Music industry organization collecting and distributing airplay and public performance royalties in the U.K. on behalf of over 3,500 record companies and 47,000 performers

- Issue licenses to U.K. radio and television stations, other broadcasters, and Internet radio stations who use sound recordings in their transmissions.

- Also license clubs, shops, pubs, restaurants, and thousands of other music users who play sound recordings in public.
- www.ppluk.com

PRS (Performing Right Society)—Collecting society for U.K. songwriters, composers, and music publishers.

- Acts as agent for its members in order to collect performing royalties whenever their musical works are performed in public, broadcast, or transmitted.
- Regardless of whether the music performed is live or by recorded means.
- Formed alliance with MCPS, who collect mechanical royalties, to form the MCPS-PRS Alliance.
- Member of CISAC.
- www.mcps-prs-alliance.co.uk

VPL (Video Performance Limited)—Represents only the copyright holders of music videos.

- Set up by the record industry in 1984.
- Currently 900 members—from the major record companies to the smallest independent—50,000 music videos are registered with them.
- Administers the right to broadcast and to publicly perform music videos, and the right to dub (i.e., copy or duplicate) music videos for both of these purposes.
- www.upluk.com

European Union

Buma/Stemra, The Netherlands—Represents the interests of music authors in the Netherlands.

- Make sure they receive remuneration for the use of their creations.
- Works for composers, lyricists, and music publishers.
- Member of CISAC.
- www.bumastemra.nl

CELAS (joint venture between PRS and GEMA).

- Exclusively represents EMI Publishing for pan-European licenses.
- Offices in the U.K. and Germany.
- www.celas.eu

GEMA (Gesellschaft für musikalische Aufführungs- und mechanische GVL [Gesellschaft zur Verwertung von Leistungsschutzrechten mbH]), Germany—Pays royalties to performers whose performances, whether as session musicians or artists, are aired on German radio and television.

- www.gvl.de

Gramex, Finland—Copyright society that promotes and administers the rights of performing artists whose performances have been recorded on phonograms and of producers of phonograms.

- Collects and distributes royalties owed.
- www.gramex.fi

GRAMO, Norway—Collects remuneration for performing artists and producers when their recordings are used for broadcasting and other public performances purposes.

- Represents performing artists and producers.
- Established in 1989.
- www.gramo.no

IMAIE (Institute for the Protection of Performing Artists), Italy—Manages the right of performing artists to receive an equal remuneration when their performances in music, cinematographic, or audiovisual works are exploited and/or broadcasted by radio and television organizations by any other user.

- Established by the trade union organizations of the performers' categories sector, created in 1977 as a free association of performing artists in order to protect their professional performances and to exercise their right to an equal remuneration.
- www.imaie.it

Musicopy, The Netherlands—Provides licenses to users for the use of sheet music (and lyrics) and pay the appropriate fee collected to the copyright owner and publisher.

- www.cedar.nl/musicopy

PPI (Phonographic Performance Ireland), Ireland—Established in 1968 to act as a central administrator of record company rights in the public performance, broadcasting, and reproduction of their recordings.

- PPI collects money when the recording or music videos are played in public and when sound recordings they have contributed to are played in public under a single license fee.
- www.ppiltd.com

SACEM (Société des auteurs, compositeurs et éditeurs de musique), France—Collects payments of authors' rights and redistributes them to the original authors and composers and the publishers.

- Stated objective is to look after the reproduction and performance rights of composers.
- Member of CISAC.
- www.sacem.fr

SCPP, France—Collects fees due to its members from sound recording and music video users and distributes these fees to copyright holders.

- Responsible for the collective administration and protection of record and video producers' rights since 1985.
- More than 1000 producers belong, including many independents and international majors including EMI, Warner, Universal, and Sony BMG.
- www.scpp.fr

SENA, The Netherlands—Appointed by the Ministry of Justice, and to the exclusion of any other, SENA has been charged with the execution of part of the Neighbouring Rights Act in 1993.

- Grants licenses to "users" of music for the public use of released phonograms for commercial purposes.
- SENA collects remunerations and, on the basis of legally approved regulations, pays them to the performing artists and record producers.
- www.sena.nl

SIAE (Italian Society of Authors and Publishers), Italy—Italian law establishes that those who wish to organize shows or entertainments where intellectual works are exploited should procure a license from SIAE and pay the relative amount.

- Established in 1882, recognized officially by copyright law of 1941.

- Presently represents well over 50,000 authors and artists.
- Member of CISAC.
- www.siae.it

STIM (Swedish Performing Right Society), Sweden—Protects the interests of authors and publishers of music in Sweden.

- On their behalf, STIM administers and licenses rights to music and text.
- Through its international network, STIM also represents rights of the worldwide repertoire of musical works.
- Member of CISAC.
- www.stim.se

SUISA (Swiss Society for the Rights of Authors of Musical Works), Switzerland—Established in 1923, it now numbers about 25,000 composers, lyricists, and music publishers.

- Collects royalties for the public use of the works in Switzerland and Liechtenstein.
- Through reciprocity agreements with over one hundred sister societies worldwide, SUISA manages the rights of two million rightsholders.
- Manages "small rights," including non-dramatic musical works, concert versions of dramatic works, and musical works for feature and television films.
- Member of CISAC.
- www.suisa.ch/en/suisa/brief

Teosto, Finland—Copyright organization for composers, lyric writers, arrangers, and music publishers.

- More than 19,000 music author and publisher members and represents some two million rightsholders around the world.
- Member of CISAC.
- www.teosto.fi

TONO, Norway—Grants license for performing music in public, collects money for the composers of music.

- Established in 1928.
- Protect the performing (financial and legal) rights of Norwegian and foreign composers, authors, and publishers of music.
- Member of CISAC.
- www.tono.no

Vervielfältigungsrechte, Germany—One of the world's leading authors' societies for works of music.

- Offer customers the worldwide repertoire of music and provide services for all music authors and rights owners.
- Member of CISAC.
- www.gema.de

ZPAV (Zwi zek Producentów Audio-Video), Poland—Founded in 1991 to represent the interests of legitimate music producers against piracy.

- Polish National Group of IFPI.
- Associates nearly one hundred industry representatives and approximately forty record companies.
- www.zpav.pl

International

BIEM (Bureau International des Sociétés Gérant les Droits D'Enregistrement et de Reproduction Mécanique)—International organization representing mechanical rights societies.

- Licenses the reproduction of songs.
- Based in France, formed in 1929.
- Represents fifty societies from fifty-three countries.
- Members of BIEM enter into agreements to allow each of them to represent the others' repertoire. In this way a BIEM society is able to license users for the vast majority of protected works in the world.
- Collaborates with the international organizations that pursue the same objective, including CISAC and GESAC.
- www.biem.org

CISAC (International Confederation of Societies of Authors and Composers)—Works toward increased recognition and protection of creators' rights.

- Founded in 1926, non-governmental, non-profit organization, headquartered in Paris.
- As of June 2007, CISAC numbered 219 authors' societies from 115 countries and indirectly represents more than 2.5 million creators within all the artistic repertoires.

- Total royalties collected by CISAC's member societies amount in 2005 to more than 6.7 billion.
- Despite the challenging environment (digital piracy, decline of CD sales, etc.), this represents a 12 percent increase since 2003.
- Main Activities and Services aim to:
  - Strengthen and develop the international network of copyright societies.
  - Secure a position for creators and their collective management organizations in the international scene.
  - Adopt and implement quality and technical efficiency criteria to increase copyright societies' interoperability.
  - Support societies' strategic development in each region and in each repertoire.
  - Retain a central database allowing societies to exchange information efficiently.
  - Participate in improving national and international copyright law and practices.
- www.cisac.org

GESAC (European Grouping of Societies of Authors and Composers)—Created in 1990, GESAC groups thirty-four of the largest authors' societies in European Union, Norway, and Switzerland.

- Represents nearly 500,000 authors or their successors in title in the areas of music, graphic and plastic arts, literary and dramatic works, and audiovisual as well as music publishers.
- www.gesac.org

IFPI (International Federation of Phonogram Industry)—Represents the recording industry worldwide, with a membership of some 1400 record companies in seventy-three countries and affiliated industry associations in forty-eight countries.

- Mission is to promote the value of recorded music, safeguard the rights of record producers, and expand the commercial uses of recorded music in all markets where its members operate.
- Members include Universal, Virgin Music, Sony BMG, EMI, and others.
- www.ifpi.org

IFRRO (International Federation of Reproduction Rights Organizations)—Established to foster the fundamental international copyright principles embodied in the Berne and Universal Copyright Conventions.

- Purpose is to facilitate, on an international basis, the collective management of reproduction and other rights relevant to copyrighted works through the cooperation of national Reproduction Rights Organizations.
- Links RROs together around the world.
- Began in 1980 as a working group of the Copyright committee of the International Publishers Association and the International Group of Scientific, Technical, and Medical Publishers.
- www.ifrro.org

A&M Records, Inc. v. Napster, 239 F.3d 1004, (9th Cir. 2001, excerpted)

Numerous guiding principles were derived from the Ninth Circuit opinion, including the following three particularly relevant guidelines:

1. The free, unlicensed downloading of a complete audio file as a "sample" does not qualify for a fair use defense.

    "5(a). Sampling.

    Napster contends that its users download MP3 files to "sample" the music in order to decide whether to purchase the recording. Napster argues that the district court: (1) erred in concluding that sampling is a commercial use because it conflated a noncommercial use with a personal use; (2) erred in determining that sampling adversely affects the market for plaintiff's copyrighted music, a requirement if the use is noncommercial; and (3) erroneously concluded that sampling is not a fair use because it determined that samplers may also engage in other infringing activity.

    The district court determined that sampling remains a commercial use even if some users eventually purchase the music. We find no error in the district court's determination. Plaintiffs have established that they are likely to succeed in proving that even authorized temporary downloading of individual songs for sampling purposes is commercial in nature. The record supports a finding that free promotional downloads are highly regulated by the record company plaintiffs and that the companies collect royalties for song samples available on retail Internet sites. Evidence relied on by the district court demonstrates that the free downloads provided by the record companies consist of thirty- to sixty-second samples or are full songs programmed to "time out," that is, exist only for a short time on the downloader's computer. In comparison, Napster users download a full, free, and permanent copy of the recording. The determination by the district court as to the commercial purpose and character of sampling is not clearly erroneous.

The district court further found that both the market for audio CDs and market for online distribution are adversely affected by Napster's service. As stated in our discussion of the district court's general fair use analysis: the court did not abuse its discretion when it found that, overall, Napster has an adverse impact on the audio CD and digital download markets. Contrary to Napster's assertion that the district court failed to specifically address the market impact of sampling, the district court determined that "even if the type of sampling supposedly done on Napster were a non-commercial use, plaintiffs have demonstrated a substantial likelihood that it would adversely affect the potential market for their copyrighted works if it became widespread."

Napster, 114 F. Supp. At 914.

The record company supports the district court's preliminary determinations that: (1) the more music that sampling users download, the less likely they are to eventually purchase the recordings on audio CD; and (2) even if the audio CD market is not harmed, Napster has adverse effects on the developing digital download market."

....

2. Napster's space-shifting is not fair use. Space-shifting—the practice of downloading an MP3 file of a track already owned on a CD for listening elsewhere—was yet another feature of the Napster service that was deemed not eligible for a fair use defense—a defense that had been successfully applied to other contexts (such as VHS videotapes).

"b. Space-shifting

Napster also maintains that space-shifting is a fair use. Space-shifting occurs when a Napster user downloads MP3 music files in order to listen to music he already owns on audio CD. Napster asserts that we have already held that space-shifting of musical compositions and sound recordings is a fair use.... We conclude that the district court did not err when it refused to apply the "shifting" analyses of Sony and Diamond. Both Diamond and Sony are inapposite because the methods of shifting in these cases did not also simultaneously involve distribution of the copyright material to the general public; the time or space-shifting of copyrighted material exposed the material only to the original user. In Diamond, for example, the copyrighted material was transferred from the user's computer hard drive to the user's portable MP3 player. So too Sony, where "the majority of VCR purchasers did not distribute taped television broadcasts, but merely enjoyed them at home."

Napster, 114 F.Supp2d at 913.

Conversely it is obvious that once a user lists a copy of music he already owns on the Napster system in order to access the music from another location, the song becomes "available to millions of other individuals," not just the original CD owner. See UMG Recordings, 92 F.Supp.2d at 351-352 (finding space-shifting of MP3 files is not a fair use even when previous ownership is demonstrated before a download is allowed)."

3. A distributor can be held to be a "vicarious infringer" for failure to control or stop infringing activities when they are financially benefiting and have the ability to supervise, but do not do so. Because Napster failed to actively police their users, the company could be held liable for vicarious infringement.

"IV.

A.   Knowledge

Contributory liability requires that the secondary infringer "know or have reason to know" of direct infringement. The district court found that Napster had both actual and constructive knowledge that its users exchanged copyrighted music. The district court also concluded that the law does not require knowledge of "specific acts of infringement" and rejected Napster's contention that because the company cannot distinguish infringing from noninfringing files, it does not "know" of the direct infringement.

It is apparent from the record that Napster has knowledge, both actual and constructive, of direct infringement. Napster claims that it is nevertheless protected from contributory liability by the teaching of Sony Corp. v. Universal City Studios, Inc. 464 U.S. 417 (1984). We disagree. We observe that Napster's actual, specific knowledge of direct infringement renders Sony's holding of limited assistance to Napster. We are compelled to make a clear distinction between the architecture of the Napster system and Napster's conduct in relation to the operational capacity of the system.

… The record supports the district court's finding that Napster has actual knowledge that specific infringing material is available using its system, that it could block access to the system by supplier of the infringing material, and that it failed to remove the material.

B. Material contribution

Under the facts as found by the district court, Napster materially contributes to the infringing activity. Relying on Fonovisa v. Cherry Auction, 76 F.Ed 259 (9th Cir.1996), the district court concluded that "without the support services defendant provides, Napster users could not find and download the music they want with the ease of which defendant boasts." Napster, 114 F.Supp.2d at 919-20 ("Napster is an integrated service designed to enable users to locate and download MP3 music files."). We agree that Napster provides "the site and facilities" for direct infringement. The district court correctly applied the reasoning in Fonovisa, and properly found that Napster materially contributes to direct infringement.

V.

We turn to the question whether Napster engages in vicarious copyright infringement. Vicarious copyright liability is an "outgrowth" of respondeat superior. Fonovisa, 76 F.3d at 262. In the context of copyright law, vicarious liability extends beyond an employer/employee relationship to cases in which a defendant "has the right and ability to supervise the infringing activity and also has a direct financial interest in such activities." Id. (quoting Gershwin, 443 F.2d at 1162); see also Polygram Int'l Publ'g, Inc. v. Nevada/TIG, Inc., 855 F. Supp. 1314, 1325-26 (D. Mass. 1994) (describing vicarious liability as a form of risk allocation).

A. Financial Benefit

The district court determined that plaintiffs had demonstrated they would likely succeed in establishing that Napster has a direct financial interest in the infringing activity. Napster, 114 F. Supp. 2d at 921-22. We agree. Financial benefit exists where the availability of infringing material "acts as a 'draw' for customers." Fonovisa, 76 F.3d at 263-64 (stating that financial benefit may be shown "where infringing performances enhance the attractiveness of a venue"). Ample evidence supports the district court's finding that Napster's future revenue is directly dependent upon "increases in user-base." More users register with the Napster system as the "quality and quantity of available music increases." 114 F. Supp. 2d at 902. We conclude that the district court did not err in determining that Napster financially benefits from the availability of protected works on its system.

B. Supervision

The district court determined that Napster has the right and ability to supervise its users' conduct. Napster, 114 F. Supp. 2d at 920-21 (finding that Napster's representations to the court regarding "its improved methods of blocking users about whom rights holders complain . . . is tantamount to an admission that defendant can, and sometimes does, police its service"). We agree in part.

The ability to block infringers' access to a particular environment for any reason whatsoever is evidence of the right and ability to supervise. See Fonovisa, 76 F.3d at 262 ("Cherry Auction had the right to terminate vendors for any reason whatsoever and through that right had the ability to control the activities of vendors on the premises."); cf. Netcom, 907 F.

Supp. at 1375-76 (indicating that plaintiff raised a genuine issue of fact regarding ability to supervise by presenting evidence that an electronic bulletin board service can suspend subscribers' accounts). Here, plaintiffs have demonstrated that Napster retains the right to control access to its system. Napster has an express reservation of rights policy, stating on its website that it expressly reserves the "right to refuse service and terminate accounts in [its] discretion, including, but not limited to, if Napster believes that user conduct violates applicable law ... or for any reason in Napster's sole discretion, with or without cause."

To escape imposition of vicarious liability, the reserved right to police must be exercised to its fullest extent. Turning a blind eye to detectable acts of infringement for the sake of profit gives rise to liability.... The district court correctly determined that Napster had the right and ability to police its system and failed to exercise that right to prevent the exchange of copyrighted material. The district court, however, failed to recognize that the boundaries of the premises that Napster "controls and patrols" are limited. *See, e.g., Fonovisa, 76 F.2d at 262-63 (in addition to having the right to exclude vendors, defendant "controlled and patrolled" the premises); see also Polygram, 855 F. Supp. at 1328-29 (in addition to having the contractual right to remove exhibitors, trade show operator reserved the right to police during the show and had its "employees walk the aisles to ensure 'rules compliance'").* Put differently, Napster's reserved "right and ability" to police is cabined by the system's current architecture. As shown by the record, the Napster system does not "read" the content of indexed files, other than to check that they are in the proper MP3 format.

Napster, however, has the ability to locate infringing material listed on its search indices, and the right to terminate users' access to the system. The file name indices, therefore, are within the "premises" that Napster has the ability to police. We recognize that the files are user-named and may not match copyrighted material exactly (for example, the artist or song could be spelled wrong). For Napster to function effectively, however, file names must reasonably or roughly correspond to the material contained in the files, otherwise no user could ever locate any desired music. As a practical *matter, Napster, its users and the record company plaintiffs have equal access to infringing material by employing Napster's "search function." Our review of the record requires us to accept the district court's conclusion that plaintiffs have demonstrated a likelihood of success on the merits of the vicarious copyright infringement claim. Napster's failure to police the system's "premises," combined with a showing that Napster financially benefits from the continuing availability of infringing files on its system, leads to the imposition of vicarious liability. We address the scope of the injunction in part VIII of this opinion."*

4. Napster attempted to raise two defenses to the infringement claim, but the court found that neither the safe harbor provision of the Digital Millennium Copyright Act protected the company from liability, nor that Napster users' actions are not protected by the Audio Home Recording Act of 1992.

"VI

Napster alleges that two statutes insulate it from liability. First, Napster asserts that its users engage in actions protected by § 1008 of the Audio Home Recording Act of 1992, 17 U.S.C. § 1008. Second, Napster argues that its liability for contributory and vicarious infringement is limited by the Digital Millennium Copyright Act, 17 U.S.C. § 512. We address the application of each statute in turn.

A. Audio Home Recording Act. . . .

We agree with the district court that the Audio Home Recording Act does not cover the downloading of MP3 files to computer hard drives. First, "[u]nder the plain meaning of the Act's definition of digital audio recording devices, computers (and their hard drives) are not digital audio recording devices because their 'primary purpose' is not to make digital audio copied recordings." Recording Indus. Ass'n of Am. v. Diamond Multimedia Sys., Inc., 180 F.3d 1072, 1078 (9th Cir. 1999). Second, notwithstanding Napster's claim that computers are "digital audio recording devices," computers do not make "digital music recordings" as defined by the Audio Home Recording Act. Id. at 1077 (citing S. Rep.

102-294) ("There are simply no grounds in either the plain language of the definition or in the legislative history for interpreting the term 'digital musical recording' to include songs fixed on computer hard drives.").

B. Digital Millennium Copyright Act

Napster also interposes a statutory limitation on liability by asserting the protections of the "safe harbor" from copyright infringement suits for "Internet service providers" contained in the Digital Millennium Copyright Act, 17 U.S.C. § 512. See Napster, 114 F. Supp. 2d at 919 n.24. The district court did not give this statutory limitation any weight favoring a denial of temporary injunctive relief. The court concluded that Napster "has failed to persuade this court that subsection 512(d) shelters contributory infringers." Id.... Plaintiffs have raised and continue to raise significant questions under this statute, including: (1) whether Napster is an Internet service provider as defined by 17 U.S.C. § 512(d); (2) whether copyright owners must give a service provider "official" notice of infringing activity in order for it to have knowledge or awareness of infringing activity on its system; and (3) whether Napster complies with § 512(i), which requires a service provider to timely establish a detailed copyright compliance policy. See A&M Records, Inc. v. Napster, Inc., No. 99-05183, 2000 WL 573136 (N.D. Cal. May 12, 2000) (denying summary judgment to Napster under a different subsection of the Digital Millennium Copyright Act, § 512(a)).

The district court considered ample evidence to support its determination that the balance of hardships tips in plaintiffs' favor:

Any destruction of Napster, Inc. by a preliminary injunction is speculative compared to the statistical evidence of massive, unauthorized downloading and uploading of plaintiffs' copyrighted works—as many as 10,000 files per second by defendant's own admission. See Kessler Dec. ¶ 29. The court has every reason to believe that, without a preliminary injunction, these numbers will mushroom as Napster users, and newcomers attracted by the publicity, scramble to obtain as much free music as possible before trial.

114 F. Supp. 2d at 926.

... VIII

The district court correctly recognized that a preliminary injunction against Napster's participation in copyright infringement is not only warranted but required. We believe, however, that the scope of the injunction needs modification in light of our opinion. Specifically, we reiterate that contributory liability may potentially be imposed only to the extent that Napster: (1) receives reasonable knowledge of specific infringing files with copyrighted musical compositions and sound recordings; (2) knows or should know that such files are available on the Napster system; and (3) fails to act to prevent viral distribution of the works. See Netcom, 907 F. Supp. at 1374-75. The mere existence of the Napster system, absent actual notice and Napster's demonstrated failure to remove the offending material, is insufficient to impose contributory liability. See Sony, 464 U.S. at 442-43.

There was a preliminary determination here that Napster users are not fair users. Uses of copyrighted material that are not fair uses are rightfully enjoined. See Dr. Seuss Enters. v. Penguin Books USA, Inc., 109 F.3d 1394, 1403 (9th Cir. 1997) (rejecting defendants' claim that injunction would constitute a prior restraint in violation of the First Amendment).

IX

...

The Copyright Act provides for various sanctions for infringers. See, e.g., 17 U.S.C. §§ 502 (injunctions); 504 (damages); and 506 (criminal penalties); see also 18 U.S.C. § 2319A (criminal penalties for the unauthorized fixation of and trafficking in sound recordings and music videos of live musical performances). These statutory sanctions represent a more than adequate legislative solution to the problem created by copyright infringement.

Imposing a compulsory royalty payment schedule would give Napster an "easy out" of this case. If such royalties were imposed, Napster would avoid penalties for any future violation of an injunction, statutory copyright damages and any possible criminal penalties for continuing infringement. The royalty structure would also grant Napster the luxury of either choosing to continue and pay royalties or shut down. On the other hand, the wronged parties would be forced to do business with a company that profits from the wrongful use of intellectual properties. Plaintiffs would lose the power to control their intellectual property: they could not make a business decision not to license their property to Napster, and, in the event they planned to do business with Napster, compulsory royalties would take away the copyright holders' ability to negotiate the terms of any contractual arrangement.

We affirm in part, reverse in part and remand. We direct that the preliminary injunction fashioned by the district court prior to this appeal shall remain stayed until it is modified by the district court to conform to the requirements of this opinion. We order a partial remand of this case on the date of the filing of this opinion for the limited purpose of permitting the district court to proceed with the settlement and entry of the modified preliminary injunction.

Even though the preliminary injunction requires modification, appellees have substantially and primarily prevailed on appeal. Appellees shall recover their statutory costs on appeal. See Fed. R. App. P. 39(a)(4) ('[i]f a judgment is affirmed in part, reversed in part, modified, or vacated, costs are taxed only as the court orders.')."

APPENDIX D

Metro-Goldwyn-Mayer Studios Inc., et al. v. Grokster, Ltd., 545 U.S. 913 (2005, excerpted)

The question addressed by the Supreme Court was "under what circumstances the distributor of a product capable of both lawful and unlawful use is liable for the acts of copyright infringement by third parties using the product." The Court described the history of the products and the companies' promotion for illegitimate purposes before holding that those who distribute and promote an object that fosters infringement can be held liable for the infringing acts of its users (third parties):

> "Grokster and StreamCast are not, however, merely passive recipients of information about infringing use. The record is replete with evidence that from the moment Grokster and StreamCast began to distribute their free software, each one clearly voiced the objective that recipients use it to download copyrighted works, and each took active steps to encourage infringement. After the notorious file-sharing service, Napster, was sued by copyright holders for facilitation of copyright infringement, A & M Records, Inc. v. Napster, Inc., 114 F. Supp. 2d 896 (ND Cal. 2000), aff'd in part, rev'd in part, 239 F. 3d 1004 (CA9 2001), StreamCast gave away a software program of a kind known as OpenNap, designed as compatible with the Napster program and open to Napster users for downloading files from other Napster and OpenNap users' computers. Evidence indicates that it was always Stream-Cast's intent to use its OpenNap network to be able to capture

*e-mail addresses of its initial target market so that it could
promote its StreamCast Morpheus interface to them, ... An
internal e-mail from a company executive stated: 'We have
put this network in place so that when Napster pulls the plug
on their free service ... or if the Court orders them shut down
prior to that ... we will be positioned to capture the flood
of their 32 million users that will be actively looking for an
alternative ...*

*Finally, there is no evidence that either company made
an effort to filter copyrighted material from users' downloads or otherwise impede the sharing of copyrighted files.
Although Grokster appears to have sent e-mails warning
users about infringing content when it received threatening
notice from the copyright holders, it never blocked anyone
from continuing to use its software to share copyrighted files.
StreamCast not only rejected another company's offer of help
to monitor infringement, but blocked the Internet Protocol
addresses of entities it believed were trying to engage in such
monitoring on its networks....*

*... The argument for imposing indirect liability in this case
is, however, a powerful one, given the number of infringing
downloads that occur every day using StreamCast's and
Grokster's software. When a widely shared service or product is
used to commit infringement, it may be impossible to enforce
rights in the protected work effectively against all direct
infringers, the only practical alternative being to go against
the distributor of the copying device for secondary liability on
a theory of contributory or vicarious infringement....*

*Evidence of active steps ... taken to encourage direct infringe-
ment, Oak Industries, Inc. v. Zenith Electronics Corp., 697 F.
Supp. 988, 992 (ND Ill. 1988), such as advertising an infringing
use or instructing how to engage in an infringing use, show an
affirmative intent that the product be used to infringe, and a
showing that infringement was encouraged overcomes the
law's reluctance to find liability when a defendant merely sells a
commercial product suitable for some lawful use, see, e.g., Water
Technologies Corp. v. Calco, Ltd., 850 F.2d 660, 668 (CA Fed. 1988)
(liability for inducement where one actively and knowingly
aids and abets another's direct infringement...). For the same
reasons that Sony took the staple-article doctrine of patent law*

as a model for its copyright safe-harbor rule, the inducement rule, too, is a sensible one for copyright. We adopt it here, holding that one who distributes a device with the object of promoting its use to infringe copyright, as shown by clear expression or other affirmative steps taken to foster infringement, is liable for the resulting acts of infringement by third parties."

....

Three features of this evidence of intent are particularly notable. First, each company showed itself to be aiming to satisfy a known source of demand for copyright infringement, the market comprising former Napster users.... Second, this evidence of unlawful objective is given added significance by MGM's showing that neither company attempted to develop filtering tools or other mechanisms to diminish the infringing activity using their software. While the Ninth Circuit treated the defendants' failure to develop such tools as irrelevant because they lacked an independent duty to monitor their users' activity, we think this evidence underscores Grokster's and StreamCast's intentional facilitation of their users infringement.... Third, there is a further complement to the direct evidence of unlawful objective. It is useful to recall that StreamCast and Grokster make money by selling advertising space, by directing ads to the screens of computers employing their software. As the record shows, the more the software is used, the more ads are sent out and the greater the advertising revenue becomes. Since the extent of the software's use determines the gain to the distributors, the commercial sense of their enterprise turns on high-volume use, which the record shows is infringing.... The unlawful objective is unmistakable.

...

In addition to intent to bring about infringement and distribution of a device suitable for infringing use, the inducement theory of course requires evidence of actual infringement by recipients of the device, the software in this case. As the account of the facts indicates, there is evidence of infringement on a gigantic scale, and there is no serious issue of the adequacy of MGM's showing on this point in order to survive the companies' summary judgment requests. Although an exact calculation of infringing use, as a basis for

*a claim of damages, is subject to dispute, there is no question
that the summary judgment evidence is at least adequate
to entitle MGM to go forward with claims for damages and
equitable relief.*"[1]

---

1 Metro-Goldwyn-Mayer Studios Inc., Et Al. v. Grokster, Ltd., 545 U.S. 913 (2005)

About the Authors

Photo: Matthew Hakola

Allen Bargfrede is a practicing entertainment and technology attorney and an assistant professor of Music Business at the Berklee College of Music. He has experience at both law firms and as corporate counsel for music and technology companies. He also serves as a marketing consultant to a number of music clients.

Allen is the author of several articles on copyright and speaks occasionally on the subject. He has experience advising music artists, record labels, managers, publishers, and producers, as well as Internet search providers and content distribution and technology companies. He holds a JD and a BA from the University of Texas and an MA from Northwestern University, and lives in Boston.

Photo: Erica Mueller

Cecily Mak is an intellectual property/digital media/entertainment law attorney with senior in-house and top tier law firm (transactional and litigation) experience. Since 2004 she has been with RealNetworks, Inc. where she currently leads the music legal team in its efforts to support the company's digital music service, Rhapsody. Previously, Cecily was an attorney at Shartsis Friese LLP, where she supported a range of large international corporations, start up businesses, and individuals. Cecily is a published author and frequent public speaker on the subject of digital media, music, and related copyright law.

In addition to working at RealNetworks, she serves as Adjunct Professor at UC Hastings where she has taught Digital Media Law, a course that is available in connection with the university's intellectual property concentration, since 2007. She lives in Marin County with her husband and their young son.

Index

Serious

about your **future** in the

music business?

If you're serious about a career in the music industry, you need more than talent. You need to know how to make your music work for you.